PRACTICAL SOCIAL WORK

Series Editor: Jo Campling

BASW

Social work is at an important stage in its development. All professions must be responsive to changing social and economic conditions if they are to meet the needs of those they serve. This series focuses on sound practice and the specific contribution which social workers can make to the well-being of our society in the 1990s.

The British Association of Social Workers has always been conscious of its role in setting guidelines for practice and in seeking to raise professional standards. The conception of the Practical Social Work series arose from a survey of BASW members to discover where they, the practitioners in social work, felt there was the most need for new literature. The response was overwhelming and enthusiastic, and the result is a carefully planned, coherent series of books. The emphasis is firmly on practice, set in a theoretical framework. The books will inform, stimulate and promote discussion, thus adding to the further development of skills and high professional standards. All the authors are practitioners and teachers of social work, representing a wide variety of experience.

JO CAMPLING

PRACTICAL SOCIAL WORK

Series Editor: Jo Campling

BASW

Robert Adams *Self-Help, Social Work and Empowerment*

David Anderson *Social Work and Mental Handicap*

James G. Barber *Beyond Casework*

Peter Beresford and Suzy Croft *Citizen Involvement: A Practical Guide for Change*

Suzy Braye and Michael Preston-Shoot *Practising Social Work Law*

Robert Brown, Stanley Bute and Peter Ford *Social Workers at Risk*

Alan Butler and Colin Pritchard *Social Work and Mental Illness*

Crescy Cannan, Lynne Berry and Karen Lyons *Social Work and Europe*

Roger Clough *Residential Work*

David M. Cooper and David Ball *Social Work and Child Abuse*

Veronica Coulshed *Management in Social Work*

Veronica Coulshed *Social Work Practice: An introduction (2nd edn)*

Paul Daniel and John Wheeler *Social Work and Local Politics*

Peter R. Day *Sociology in Social Work Practice*

Lena Dominelli *Anti-Racist Social Work: A Challenge for White Practitioners and Educators*

Celia Doyle *Working with Abused Children*

Angela Everitt, Pauline Hardiker, Jane Littlewood and Audrey Mullender *Applied Research for Better Practice*

Kathy Ford and Alan Jones *Student Supervision*

David Francis and Paul Henderson *Working with Rural Communities*

Michael D. A. Freeman *Children, their Families and the Law*

Alison Froggatt *Family Work with Elderly People*

Danya Glaser and Stephen Frosh *Child Sexual Abuse*

Bryan Glastonbury *Computers in Social Work*

Gill Gorell Barnes *Working with Families*

Cordelia Grimwood and Ruth Popplestone *Women, Management and Care*

Jalna Hanmer and Daphne Statham *Women and Social Work: Towards a Woman-Centred Practice*

Tony Jeffs and Mark Smith (eds) *Youth Work*

Michael Kerfoot and Alan Butler *Problems of Childhood and Adolescence*

Mary Marshall *Social Work with Old People (2nd edn)*

Paula Nicolson and Rowan Bayne *Applied Psychology for Social Workers (2nd edn)*

Kieran O'Hagan *Crisis Intervention in Social Services*

Michael Oliver *Social Work with Disabled People*

Joan Orme and Bryan Glastonbury *Care Management: Tasks and Workloads*

Lisa Parkinson *Separation, Divorce and Families*

Malcolm Payne *Social Care in the Community*

Malcolm Payne *Working in Teams*

John Pitts *Working with Young Offenders*

Michael Preston-Shoot *Effective Groupwork*

Carole R. Smith *Adoption and Fostering: Why and How*

Carole R. Smith *Social Work with the Dying and Bereaved*

Carole R. Smith, Marty T. Lane and Terry Walsh *Child Care and the Courts*

Gill Stewart and John Stewart *Social Work and Housing*

Neil Thompson *Anti-Discriminatory Practice*

Derek Tilbury *Working with Mental Illness*

Alan Twelvetrees *Community Work (2nd edn)*

Hilary Walker and Bill Beaumont (eds) *Working with Offenders*

Working with Young Offenders

John Pitts

First published 1990 by
THE MACMILLAN PRESS LTD
Houndmills, Basingstoke, Hampshire RG21 2XS
and London
Companies and representatives
throughout the world

ISBN 0–333–46398–6 hardcover
ISBN 0–333–46399–4 paperback

A catalogue record for this book is available
from the British Library.

Printed in Hong Kong

Reprinted 1993

'I want to be valued, in ways that I am not: I want to be more than valuable . . . I want to steal something.' — Margaret Atwood, *The Handmaid's Tale*

'Anyway, I keep picturing all these little kids playing some game in some big field of rye and all. Thousands of little kids, and nobody's around – nobody big, I mean – except me. And I'm standing on the edge of some crazy cliff. What I have to do, I have to catch everybody if they start to go over the cliff – I mean if they're running and they don't look where they're going I have to come out of somewhere and *catch* them. That's all I'd do all day. I'd just be the catcher in the rye and all. I know it's crazy, but that's the only thing I'd really like to be. I know it's crazy.' — J. D. Salinger, *The Catcher in the Rye*

Contents

Preface

This book is aimed at non-specialist social workers who, amongst other things, work with children and young people in trouble. I have assumed that they will have some understanding of the basic concepts and assumptions which underly the practice of casework, family work, social group work and community work. I have tried to identify the issues, skills and procedures specific to work in the juvenile justice system which a thoughtful social worker, confronted with a 'juvenile', would find most useful.

In the course of writing this book I have talked with many people, some of whom specialize in work with young offenders and some of whom do not. I asked workers and students with little experience of working with young offenders what they thought they needed to know, and I asked specialists what they thought workers with young offenders should know.

The inexperienced were unsure about what they needed to know but were aware of the conflicting pressures upon workers in the system. The experienced were adamant that social workers needed to understand the procedures and politics of the juvenile justice system, to take little at face value, and to be prepared to stick their necks out for children and young people in trouble. They wanted social workers to have done their homework and not to fall into the traps which the juvenile justice system sets for the unwary. They wanted them to have the resilience to operate in the real world of staff shortages, rate-capping and of 'law and order'.

I said that this sounded like a tall order and a tough job and when they agreed I asked them why they continued to do it. They were astounded by my question. Was I suggesting that there might be a choice? What else could anybody possibly want to do? And I was struck once again by the commitment of people who work with children and young people in trouble and by the fascination that this work holds for them. Working with young offenders is like that and the hardest part of writing this book has been to convey what 'that' is like.

I have been helped in this attempt by a lot of people. Dave Crimmins and Jane Linklater are the two most experienced workers with young offenders that I know. They have, over time, become a sort of professional 'gang in my head' and I find that I cannot write for any length of time without wondering what they would have said. I am indebted to Dave for reading drafts of this book and to Jane for her advice on family work with young offenders. At the West London Institute, discussions in the staff group and in my social work group have been an important source of 'real' material. I am grateful to Sue Barclay, Anne Ettienne, Kevin Jones, Anne Marshal and Procespina Young who gave their ideas, and their group tutorial as well, to help be become clearer about the ways social workers use their intuition and why some young people apparently want to go to prison.

My daughter Lisa Pitts pointed out that the book was most interesting when it concerned what people felt about things and she also drew my attention to the boring bits, most of which I hope I have now deleted. Beyond this she introduced me to the novels of, and letters to, Judy Blume which have proved to be an invaluable source of the 'real' experiences of 'real' young people. My sons, Matthew and Adrian, simply continued to demonstrate how reasonable, relaxed and balanced young people so often seem in comparison with their elders.

Deborah has read the various versions of this book and our conversations have helped me to clarify what I was trying to say. It was Deborah who pointed out the dangers of confusing the world of the textbook with the real world in which overstretched social workers do the best they can with what they've got. I hope that I have been able to convey something of the realities of this world but also something of how enjoyable it is to work with young offenders.

JOHN PITTS

1

Introduction: The Politics of Policy

> Even the Aylesbury police have failed to find the horrors listed by Mr. Hurd. 'It's certainly not out of control here. If anything its got better than a few years ago', says Inspector Ray Henderson. 'Everyone's just jumped on the young people and drink bandwagon, but I have to tell you that the last two drunks we arrested on public order offences were both 38. I just wish the Home Secretary hadn't opened his big mouth.' (Kate Muir, *Guardian*, 10 August 1988.)

It quickly becomes evident to anybody who works with young offenders that they are involved in a system, a nexus of laws, institutions and practices which is quite unlike the systems they confront in work with other clients. It is not just that magistrates and the police hold a great deal of power in the juvenile justice system; they do in child-care as well. Nor is it that social workers feel subject to political and media pressure to respond to the 'bad' behaviour of young offenders. This pressure is also there in cases of non-accidental injury to children. The difference concerns the *social value* and the *political significance* attributed to children and the young people in trouble.

The social value of young offenders

The social value placed upon any group of people is determined, in part, by the level at which decisions about them are made. If, as has been the case in the late 1980s, key policy decisions about children at risk of death from non-accidental injury are made in the Cabinet, this alerts us to the importance of their plight. If, however, as has been the case with pensioners at risk of death from hypothermia, a junior government minister merely enjoins their relatives to knit them a woolly hat, then an equally clear, but opposite, message about their social value is delivered. The attribution of social value will dictate the numbers of people who write books, or make television documentaries about the group in question, which in turn determines the extent to which their predicament will infuse public consciousness.

It is clear that young offenders have little social value. Cases in which children, who are the responsibility of social workers, are either seriously assaulted or killed invariably become front page news. When children and young people who are the responsibility of prison department personnel are seriously assaulted or killed in custody, as in the case of the deaths at Glenochil detention centre (DC) between 1981 and 1984 and the criminal assaults investigated at Aldington and Send DCs in 1985 and 1986, it seldom if ever evokes more than a few column inches on the inside pages of the newspapers, and a ministerial denial (Pitts, 1988). It is a salutary thought that virtually everybody involved in social work knows of Tyra Henry and Jasmine Beckford, while hardly anybody has heard of Angus Boyd. Angus Boyd was found dead in his cell at Glenochil DC on 17 February 1984. He was the fifth boy to die there in three years and, like the others, he was the subject of strict 'suicide observation' at the time of his death. The dereliction of duty, the abuse of adult power and the impact of the blows is the same as in cases of non-accidental injury to children. It is the social value of the victims which is different.

While their low social value determines that the treatment of young offenders is rarely subject to the kind of media and public scrutiny reserved for children in danger, their political significance ensures that they receive much more than their fair share of a different kind of attention.

The political significance of young offenders

The ultimate aim of Labour Party juvenile justice policies in the 1960s was to take the issue of juvenile crime off the political agenda and place it on an agenda of social anomalies to be eradicated by the scientifically informed interventions of the 'trained experts' employed by the local authority social services departments. The attempt was made to recast the image of the delinquent as the innocent victim of social and psychological pressures in order to shift the political focus away from the offender and onto the social and psychological factors which precipitated his offending. In its attempt to do this it encountered sustained resistance from the Conservative opposition and the legal and academic establishments.

This attempt to decriminalise and depoliticise the juvenile justice system was unsuccessful. Those sections of the 1969 Children and Young Persons Act (CYPA) which threatened the power and supremacy of the bench and the judiciary, although they had been passed by parliament, were not implemented by the Heath administration of 1970. Indeed, as the decade progressed we witnessed the steady 're-politicisation' of 'youth' in general and young offenders in particular. From 1979 this tendency became an established fact of political life to the point where it seemed that the privatisation of nationalised industries must inevitably be accompanied by the nationalisation of private morality. This 'repoliticisation' of 'youth' was part of a political strategy developed in response to an economic problem (Taylor, 1981).

The restructuring of western economies in the last two decades has created serious problems for governments. As the numbers of those in work who are able to contribute to the costs of health and welfare services and state benefits has declined, the size of the 'unproductive' population, which depends on these services, has grown. This fiscal crisis has been exacerbated by tax cuts, an ageing population which is making increasing demands upon state services, and a political reluctance to commit a larger proportion of the gross national product to those services.

A by-product of this situation is an assumed, and sometimes actual, rise in levels of crime and social disorder among those marginal social groups who bear the brunt of economic fluctuations and whose already meagre opportunities are further eroded in periods of high unemployment (Lee and Young, 1984). In these circumstances British governments have developed a dual strategy to deal with the financial and control problems posed by these 'unproductive' elements. They have pursued policies aimed at what Spitzer (1975) describes as the redistribution of 'social junk' and the control of 'social dynamite'. Box (1983) writes:

> In response to this fiscal crisis, governments have attempted to pursue a policy of *decarceration*, that is, removing people from mental hospitals and similar institutions, closing them down and diverting potential inmates by encouraging 'community treatment', which happens to be comparatively cheaper. The latter group present a more intractable problem because they are actually or potentially more troublesome. Spitzer argues that this problem population – the able-bodied, mainly young unemployed and unemployable – throws into question the ability of the capitalist mode of production to generate enough work and wealth and this helps contribute to a situation conducive to the creation of a legitimacy crisis (p. 209).

Their low social value notwithstanding, some groups of young people, regarded as socially volatile, have been subject to higher levels of surveillance and intervention in the 1970s and 1980s (Hall *et al.*, 1978 and Lee and Young, 1984). This in turn led to harsher sentencing and, as a result, the early 1980s witnessed a surge in the numbers of young people entering penal establishments. In their attempts to resolve the consequent 'prison crisis' governments have resorted to the introduction of bifurcated juvenile justice policies (Bottoms, 1977).

Bifurcation

Bifurcation is a legislative strategy which allows governments to have their law and order cake while they eat their public expenditure one too. Bifurcated policies redescribe, and then redistribute, deviant populations. Some categories of offenders are represented as more serious and menacing while others, who had previously been regarded as a threat, are represented as relatively unproblematic. The activity of a small number of offenders is dramatised while that of others is 'normalised'. The stock in trade of bifurcated policies is the transformation of junk into dynamite and vice-versa.

Bifurcated policies increase the penalties imposed upon the dramatised group while reducing those imposed upon the normalised group. These policies often involve the development of community-based alternatives to residential care or custody for groups of newly normalised offenders who were previously incarcerated.

The 1982 Criminal Justice Act (CJA) reduced the minimum period a child or young person could spend in a detention centre to three weeks. This was accompanied by a great deal of Home Office public relations activity bent upon demonstrating that if young offenders were subjected to the new, tougher regimes for shorter periods the deterrent effect would be greater. It encouraged magistrates to make greater use of this 'new' sentencing option and, in anticipation of the success of its initiative, it warned the governors of the centres to prepare themselves for a 40 per cent increase in throughput. The implementation of this section of the Act in 1983 was accompanied by an investment of £15 000 000 by Leon Brittan the Home Secretary in 4500 'alternatives to custody' for persistent young offenders and an attendant flurry of PR activity from the DHSS and the Home Office. The government was trying to persuade magistrates to sentence larger numbers of less problematic children and young people, whom they described as 'hooligans', to a very brief and relatively inexpensive spell 'inside'. They were also trying to persuade magistrates simultaneously to divert a similar number of more serious young offenders, who attracted much longer and much more expensive custodial sentences, and who constituted an important element in the 'prison crisis', to alternatives to custody in the community.

Bifurcated policies have met with only limited success because they have been introduced by governments which have been unwilling to limit the power or discretion of the bench or the judiciary. Box and Hale (1986) argue that this is because:

> governments faced with a population they perceive to be increasingly ungovernable, and realising that their economic policies may substantially exacerbate this, particularly amongst certain sections of the community, have not seen any pragmatic sense in alienating such a trusted and loyal ally as the judiciary, or abandoning prison as an iron fist of threat, control and punishment (p. 93).

Judges and magistrates always seem to grasp the first message of the bifurcated policy: that they should get tough on some offenders, but the second message, that they should simultaneously go easy on others, seems to elude them. This is one of the major reasons why, over the period, we have usually seen the parallel growth of youth imprisonment and its alternative.

The attraction of bifurcated juvenile justice policies to law and order governments is that they appear to offer a means whereby

Conservative theory's explanations of, and solutions to, the related problems of juvenile crime and economic recession can be put into operation without incurring inordinate costs.

Conservative theory

Traditionally, although Conservative theory's explanation of crime and civil disorder has been somewhat lacking in intellectual refinement it has served as an article of faith and a rallying cry for the Conservative party's rank and file. Conservative theory locates juvenile crime as a manifestation of the deeper problem of moral decline which is seen to generate not only law-breaking but industrial strife and inflation as well. This moral degeneracy is a consequence of misguided government welfare initiatives of the past and the relaxation of moral standards which they have fostered. These policies have resulted in the disruption and dislocation of the moral order and 'the spread of what could be called a delinquent syndrome, a conglomeration of behaviour, speech, appearance and attitudes, a frightening ugliness and hostility which pervades human interaction, a flaunting of contempt for other human beings, a delight in crudity, cruelty and violence, a desire to challenge and humiliate but never, but never to please' (Morgan, 1978, p. 13).

For conservative theory delinquent 'youth' is an ideological device with a dual significance. On one hand the 'bad' behaviour of the young is a consequence of the mistakes made by the parental generation, while on the other it indicates the reprehensible direction in which our society is moving.

Norman Tebbit (1986) located the source of the violence and fecklessness of contemporary youth in the negative attitudes to authority, morality and hard work developed by their parents in the 'permissive '60s'. In this scenario the 'sins' and omissions of the fathers can be clearly identified in the deficiencies of their sons and daughters. The bad attitudes of one generation are translated, lock stock and barrel, it seems, into the bad behaviour of the next.

For Conservative theory the moral and economic spheres are one and economic success is both a consequence and a manifestation of moral worth. The task for government is to turn the clock back to a time when the natural economic disciplines of the free market and the natural moral disciplines of common sense ensured that the industrious and the thrifty reaped their rewards while cheats, thieves and idlers received their just deserts. As a result, in the period from 1970, Conservative governments which claimed to be arresting economic recession have always embarked simultaneously upon symbolic crusades to arrest moral decline amongst 'youth'.

These moral crusades have identified 'youth' as the target of, and the educational and juvenile justice systems as the site for, the confrontation. The moral crusades and bifurcated policies which have flowed from the account of the social world given by conservative theory have generated the irrationality to which the juvenile justice system in England and Wales is heir.

Irrational social policy

If we trace the history of young offender legislation in England and Wales from the 1970s we encounter laws, policies and practices which are at best contradictory and at worst irrational and damaging. The legislation, far from offering a rational response to the problems experienced by children and young people in trouble with the law, their victims, and those who work with them, often compounds these very problems. Many of the changes in young offender legislation from the early 1970s onwards have been made in the face of research evidence which indicated that the intended change would either contribute nothing to the achievement of the government's stated objectives or would actually make the problem, to which the legislation was the government's intended solution, worse.

At the Conservative Party conference in October 1979 William Whitelaw announced the introduction of a new experimental regime, the 'short sharp shock', at New Hall and Send detention centres. The centres were opened in 1980. In March 1981 the experiment was extended to another two centres. In 1984 the Home Office Young Offender Psychology Unit which evaluated the effectiveness of the new centres published *Tougher Regimes in Detention Centres*. The purpose of the experiment had been, it said, to see whether young offenders could effectively be dettered from committing further offences by spending a period of weeks in a detention centre with 'a more rigorous and demanding regime'. The report noted however that: 'The introduction of the pilot project regimes had no discernible effect on the rate at which trainees were reconvicted' (Home Office, 1984, p. 243). On 5 March 1985 the new regime was extended to all detention centres in England and Wales.

The case of the short, sharp, shock is one of many examples of a British government implementing a juvenile justice policy which, according to research evidence and the opinions of its professional advisers at the Home Office and the DHSS, was destined to fail. David Farrington, reflecting upon the contribution research has made to the formulation and monitoring of government juvenile justice policies observes that 'It is tempting to think that the government, the Home Office and the Department of Health and Social Security do not want an adequate evaluation of their juvenile justice activities' (Farrington, 1984).

In as much as social scientific research can ever 'prove' anything it has proved that locking-up children and young people in detention centres, community homes, young offender institutions and prisons in an attempt to change their delinquent behaviour has been an expensive failure. Yet as more and more studies have demonstrated the tendency of these institutions to increase the reconviction rates of their ex-inmates, to evoke violence from previously non-violent people, to render ex-inmates effectively unemployable, to destroy family relationships and to put a potentially victimised citizenry at greater risk, so the populations of these institutions have grown.

If we wish to understand the persistence of irrationality in the juvenile justice system we have to understand its importance to 'law and order' politicians as a forum in which they can demonstrate that they are arresting the decline in moral standards. This endeavour assumes the political significance it does because in Conservative theory it is declining moral standards which are at the root of all the other social and economic problems afflicting the nation. As a result the shape of the juvenile justice system in England and Wales in a 'law and order' era is determined ultimately neither by an informed understanding of the needs and difficulties of the juveniles who pass through it, nor a commitment to justice, but by the pursuit of political legitimacy.

2

Negative Practice

As we have seen, there was a time when it appeared that the juvenile justice system might be separated from the system of political legitimation. The reforms pioneered by the Wilson administration, which culminated in the 1969 CYPA and the 1970 Social Services (Reorganisation) Act, were an attempt to remove the young offender from the criminal justice arena and juvenile crime from the political agenda. These initiatives, informed by the research of some of the most eminent British social scientists of the day, created the administrative basis and the theoretical rationale for the parallel development of local authority social services departments and professional social work. Beyond the 'scientific' rationality of this endeavour, however, lay what Booker (1980) describes as 'The Utopian belief that, through drastic social and political reorganisation, aided by the greater use of State planning, we should be able to create an entirely new kind of just, fair and equal society'. It was an optimistic ideology predicated upon a belief that the intrinsic altruism and goodness of human beings could be realised if the fruits of a perpetually expanding economy could be scientifically targeted on social problems. When, in the late 1960s and early 1970s, the economy went into recession and it became clear that Britain could be entering the kind of protracted economic crisis which the dominant, Keynesian, explanations of economic life maintained were no longer possible, doubt was cast upon the entire reforming enterprise.

The recession which began at the end of the 1960s quite literally marked the end of an era in the development of the Welfare State. As the 1970s progressed, the optimism of the Wilson years was supplanted by a mood of pessimism as successive governments struggled to come to grips with a steadily worsening economic crisis. This pessimism was reflected in social and criminal justice policies; in the theories developed by social scientists and in the practices adopted by professional workers. Expenditure cuts, staff shortages, frozen posts and unallocated cases became the reality of the social services departments, designed only a few years earlier to bring a comprehensive system of care and support to citizens in need.

These problems were compounded by an increasingly strident attack on the reforms of the 1960s and their consequences. Workers with young offenders were singled out for a particularly vitriolic political, theoretical and media assault. This backlash was the more disconcerting because it came from across the entire political spectrum. By the mid- to late-1970s the critique of social work with children and young people in trouble had consolidated into a new, pessimistic, theoretical and political orthodoxy (cf. Berlins and Wansell, 1974; Morgan, 1978; and Morris *et al.*, 1980). This was a critique to which (the theory and practice of) social work with young offenders is still trying to find an adequate rejoinder. The critique came from five main sources.

1. Slump politics (Conservative theory)

As we have already noted, the slump politics generated by Conservative theory identified the victims of the economic recession as its cause and found in the behaviour of young offenders the example par excellence of what was wrong with the country. This attempt to transform the economic crisis into a moral one generated criminal justice policies which increasingly required workers with young offenders to justify themselves in terms of their capacity to exert control over, rather than to offer help and support to, children and young people in trouble.

2. The liberal justice lobby

Emerging first in the USA in the mid-1960s but gaining ground in Britain by the mid-1970s the liberal justice lobby attacked the social work presence in the juvenile justice system for its capacity to make unwarranted incursions into the lives and liberties of children and young people in trouble. Characterising the social enquiry report as a 'character assassination' and pouring scorn upon professional social work's claims to any specialised knowledge or expertise, the argument was often long on rhetoric but short in evidence and analysis (cf. Morris *et al.*, 1980). Social workers were to be barred from the courts and solicitors and magistrates armed only with their law books and good common sense were to defend working-class young offenders against the rampant professional entrepreneurialism of social work.

3. *Right-wing criminology*

Coming initially from the USA but eagerly appropriated by the British right-wing intelligentsia the critique suggested that while social science may have accurately identified the social and economic conditions which generate crime, as a society we lacked both the political will and the technical knowledge to address these conditions. We should content ourselves, it argued, with policies which strove to minimise the impact of crime and incapacitate the criminal. This would involve giving the courts and the police the necessary powers to take action and, one of its consequences would be a minimisation of the quasi-judicial discretion exercised by people like social workers. This position differs from that of the liberal justice lobby in that right-wing criminology is more interested in strengthening the capacity of the justice system to exert control over criminals than with extending their legal rights. What they share with the liberal justice lobby however is a desire to get social workers out of the courtroom.

4. *Left-wing criminology*

The right-wing criminological critique identified the social work presence in the justice system as a barrier to the establishment of justice. The liberal justice lobby saw it as an example of the tendency of public agencies to make unwarranted incursions into the lives and liberties of citizens. Paradoxically the critique developed by left-wing criminology was effectively in agreement with both of them, albeit for substantially different reasons. In addition it indicted social work as the velvet glove disguising the iron fist of capitalist oppression. In this account social workers were unwitting agents who served only to blunt the edge, or blurr the reality, of class domination. In its softer version, the left-wing critique located social workers as the 'zookeepers' of deviance who imposed pernicious deviant labels upon people who were merely engaged in relatively innocuous behaviour, which was perfectly acceptable in its own cultural milieu. Whether they were postponing the revolution by promoting false consciousness amongst their clients, or lurching clumsily through the social world imposing pejorative labels upon already disadvantaged people, the left-wing criminological critique located social workers as part of the problem rather than part of the solution.

5. *Conventional criminology*

The mid-1970s witnessed the abandonment by conventional criminology of its central project, the investigation of the causes of crime and the development of techniques to 'cure' or eradicate it. In the light of all the available scientific evidence the criminological establishment came reluctantly to the view that, like the search for the philosopher's stone, the quest for an effective method of rehabilitating criminals was probably a lost cause. This watershed, termed 'the decline of the rehabilitative ideal', signalled a profound change in the concerns of conventional criminology.

In this period it moved from its attempt to discover the causes of crime to the far less ambitious project of devising more effective methods of processing and managing ajudicated criminals. One of the by-products of this change was to highlight the ineffectiveness of social work as a means of stopping people committing crimes. This effectively put an end to the relationship which had previously been assumed to exist between criminologists and social workers. The assumption that criminology would develop a correctional technology which the social work technician would then put into operation had to be abandoned. The 'decline of the rehabilitative ideal' removed an important theoretical prop from the practice of social work with offenders and threatened to leave social workers without a job to do in the criminal justice system.

To sum up, for right-wing criminology the primary function of social work in the justice system was to impede judges and the police in their highly popular attempts to offer protection to a potentially victimised citizenry. Slump politics made it clear that if social work was to retain a role in the juvenile justice system in a 'law and order' era it must stop colluding with the bad behaviour of its clients and start exerting far more control over them. Left-wing criminology and the liberal justice lobby argued that it was already doing this anyway and bamboozling its clients as well. Conventional criminology wasn't quite sure what social work was doing in the justice system but it was sure that whatever it was, it didn't work.

Criminologists, policy-makers and radical politicians of the right, left and centre, were no longer interested in the social, psychological or existential antecedents of offending which had been the primary focus of social work with offenders in the 1950s and 1960s. From the mid-1970s the debate about young offenders in Britain moved from a preoccupation with the causes of juvenile crime to a concern about its effects. Questions of victimisation and the effectiveness of sentencing supplanted questions of motivation.

Negative practice

Social workers on the receiving end of this barrage were left with no crumbs of comfort. Their theoretical base and the skills and methods they had been using in their work with children and young people in trouble had been systematically demolished by 'friends' and enemies alike. Meanwhile the 1969 CYPA had given them even greater responsibility for young offenders. In consequence the social work practice which emerged in the wake of the critique was defensive; concerned to cause less harm rather than to do more good. The new orthodoxy of 'radical non-intervention' offered a way forward for social workers, bombarded by theorists with 'evidence' that their endeavours had apparently worsened the problems to which they had hoped to be a solution (Schur, 1974). Apprehension about intervention and pressure from rapidly growing caseloads, in which young offenders assumed an ever-lower priority, often resulted in 'radical non-intervention' by default.

Whether by default or by design, however, social work with young offenders in the mid- to late 1970s came to observe Schur's injunction that whenever and wherever possible we should 'leave the kids alone'. The collapse of confidence induced by the discovery of the destructive potential of social work interventions in the lives of young offenders and pressure from higher priority work were two important reasons why many local authority social services departments adopted minimalist young offender strategies. 'Preventive work' with youngsters 'at risk' of future delinquency was rejected because of its perceived propensity to widen the net of control and draw new, previously unidentified, populations into the system. Instead the idea that we should invervene only with ajudicated offenders became established as the cornerstone of the minimalist orthodoxy which pervaded the theory and the practice of social work with young offenders in the 1970s and 1980s. This minimalism found expression in five main areas:

1. Systems management

Systems management exercises became increasingly popular with hard-pressed local authority social services departments in the late-1970s as they confronted the enormous cost of holding young offenders in residential establishments. Systems management and intervention is the attempt to change the behaviour of key decision-makers in the juvenile justice system in order that penalties imposed upon young offenders are minimised and, as a result, the number of children and young people committed to care and custody is reduced. In the longer term, residential establishments for young offenders are closed, and community-based alternatives are established to respond to their erstwhile populations. The system is monitored and a computerised analysis reveals the points at which the 'wrong decisions' are being made. 'Gatekeeping' procedures, aimed at exerting control over maverick decision-makers, are then instituted in order to iron out the anomalies and return the system to a state of rationality (cf. Thorpe, 1980).

This approach to problems in the juvenile justice system has been fairly effective in reducing the numbers of juvenile offenders referred to residential establishments by social workers but, until the mid-1980s, it was having a much less significant impact upon decisions made by the police and the juvenile bench who, as Parker (1980) has noted, hold substantially more power in the system than social workers.

As we shall see, work pioneered by the NACRO Juvenile

Offenders Team (JOT) developed a form of systems intervention in the mid-1980s, which had the kind of impact upon custodial sentencing which had eluded earlier attempts to manage systems from a base within the social services department (NACRO, 1987). The JOT approach to diversion had an important impact on the ways in which projects funded by the 1983 DHSS/Home Office 'New Initiative' in Intermediate Treatment (IT) were established and managed. In areas where these projects operated levels of custodial sentencing were often reduced substantially. IT was introduced in the C&YP Act 1969 to provide an intervention which was more intensive than individual supervision in the community by a social worker yet less disruptive than removal to residential care. (The role of IT in the juvenile justice system is dealt with in Chapter 8.) Early IT developed interventions which attempted to respond to the educational, recreational and social needs of youngsters in trouble. The systems management initiatives of the late 1970s, by contrast, strove to persuade the key system decision-makers, the police, social workers and magistrates, to intervene as little as possible. A major weapon in this battle against prosecution and incarceration was the alternative tariff.

The alternative tariff

If juvenile court magistrates were to use the community-based alternatives, established in the wake of systems management initiatives, as a sentencing option, it was argued, the alternative had to offer a programme and a regime which acknowledged their concerns. These concerns were assumed to centre on the importance of the child or young person being made to confront their offending in a situation which offered a heightened level of control and surveillance. It was these assumptions which set the scene for the introduction of 'tracking' and the 'correctional curriculum'.

Tracking is a method of intensive surveillance in which the young offenders agree to a contract which specifies where they will be, and when they will be there, for the duration of their programme. The tracker then appears, usually unannounced, at places where the young offenders are supposed to be to make sure that they are there. Beyond this the tracker will keep in touch with parents, teachers and other interested adults in order to check on progress in the areas of education, relationships and recreation. Should the young persons not be where they are supposed to be or not be making progress in the specified areas they can be taken into the tracking headquarters for a more intensive day-care programme which will address the problems they are having in behaving correctly.

Tracking was developed in the USA as an alternative response to serious offenders who would otherwise have spent long periods in jail. One of the criticisms of tracking schemes in Britain has been that in applying the approach to less serious offenders tracking actually increases rather than decreases the level of control to which they would otherwise be subjected.

The correctional curriculum is another US import. Based on theories of human motivation developed within behavioural psychology it comprises a set of techniques which strive to enable the offender to identify the moments in the behavioural sequence, which culminated in the delinquent act, when they might have acted differently. Through role-play, 'cartooning' and video feedback young offenders are encouraged to become attuned to those features of social situations which evoke a criminal behavioural response from them. The programme then attempts to de-sensitise them to these stimuli while inculcating alternative behavioural triggers which evoke non-criminal responses to criminogenic situations. In its pure form the correctional curriculum, like tracking, is unconcerned with questions of social need or educational or emotional deprivation. To do so, it is claimed, would be to engage in the kind of spurious 'needology' so beloved of conventional social work (Thorpe, 1980). Many workers who operate a correctional curriculum do in fact take an interest in, and try to help young offenders with these other aspects of their lives but such 'help' is not a central feature of the correctional programme.

Whether tracking or the correctional curriculum will be shown to have made a greater impact upon offending behaviour than any other intervention is less significant than the fact that they offer the juvenile bench a set of alternative penalties designed, in terms of duration and content, to replicate existing institutional penalties. Ultimately it is as strategic initiatives which aim to change the behaviour of juvenile court magistrates and as cost-effective responses to individual offenders that they should be evaluated.

3. The individualisation of practice

The emergence of systems management and the alternative tariff are examples of the way that the advent of minimalism marked a change in the level at which social phenomena and social problems were analysed and in the kinds of theorists who were doing the analysis. During the 1960s in Britain and the USA social policies in the sphere of juvenile crime and justice were profoundly influenced by the opportunity theory developed by Richard Cloward and Lloyd Ohlin (1960). What the theorists strove to identify and what governments strove, through their social policies, to address, were the ultimate causes of crime and social deprivation. As we have seen, by the mid-1970s a new breed of theorists and policy-makers were rejecting such optimistic endeavours and opting instead for policies in which the minimum amount of state intervention would make the maximum quantifiable impact. It was in the pursuit of this endeavour that these 'New Realists' lighted upon individual incapacitation as a response to, and individual wickedness as an explanation of, predatory crime. Platt and Takagi (1981) write:

> There is general agreement among the new realists that wicked people exist. Nothing avails but to set them apart from innocent people. And many people, neither wicked nor innocent, but watchful, dissembling, and calculating of their opportunities, ponder our reactions to wickedness as a cue to what they might profitably do. We have trifled with the wicked, made sport of the innocent, and encouraged the calculators (pp. 46–7).

It is not difficult to see why the analytical individualism of New Realism came to establish the boundaries of the contemporary discourse on juvenile crime and justice. It was assisted in its task by criminologists of ostensibly different political persuasions who not only posed no alternative to New Realism but, as we have noted, actually echoed in oblique ways what the new realists were saying far more coherently.

The changed parameters of the debate about crime meant that agencies and professional workers with young offenders were required to justify their activity much more in terms of its contribution to the eradication of crime than its contribution to neighbourhood resources or the social and psychological well-being of the offender. In short, workers and agencies were under increasing pressure to offer 'hard-headed', 'no nonsense' responses to children and young people in trouble irrespective of their needs or, indeed, what might actually work.

In practice this meant that neighbourhood strategies based around clubs or adventure playgrounds, detached (street) work with natural groups of young people, and community work initiatives which attempted to enable the children, young people and adults who lived in high crime-rate inner-city areas to gain more power and control over decisions which affected their lives were called into question. These relatively expensive attempts to address criminogenic social conditions, and their consequences, through compensatory programmes and interventions in social and political structures had, by and large, run out of steam and funding by the mid-1970s (cf. Smith, 1972; and Robins and Cohen, 1978). In 1976 an entire phrase of 'Urban Aid' funding, a major element in the British Poverty programme, was redesignated to assist local authorities to establish Intermediate Treatment Centres. This was one of many signals that central and local government were getting out of the 'social compensation' business and into cost-effective social reaction.

The change in the focus of practice away from the structural social disadvantages and the cultural needs of young people at risk and in trouble, to time-limited responses to individual ajudicated offenders required a radically different theoretical underpinning.

4. The renaissance of behaviourism

After two and a half decades in which positivism in general, and behavioural approaches to human psychology in particular, were subjected to a sustained assault within the social sciences, behaviourism suddenly made a comeback in the mid-1970s. For the social work profession, which by this time was tending to draw its intellectual sustenance from theories derived from the psychodynamics of Freud and Jung, the general systems theory of Ludwig von Bertalanffy and the structural analyses of Marx and Durkheim, this renaissance was not altogether welcome. One of the reasons for its cool reception in most quarters was that behaviourism tended to leave the most interesting things that human beings did, unexplained. Another was that behaviourism conceived of a much more modest role for social workers than they would have chosen for themselves.

Its sudden return did not indicate that behaviourists had spent their wilderness years thinking up good arguments with which to confound their critics. On the contrary, they had just kept on doing the thing they did best, namely, the quantitative analysis of the biological bases of behaviour. Behaviourism's sudden return was attributable not to the compelling explanatory power of its arguments but to convenience. Behaviourism, unlike other approaches to individual and social problems developed in the social sciences, fitted in with the new minimalist orthodoxy of juvenile justice. Stan Cohen (1983) writes:

> Here is where the new behaviourism appears: it offers the modest prospect of changing behaviours rather than people, of altering situations and physical environments rather than the social order. To be sure, the pure Skinnerian model was a highly ambitious one: a totally synchronised predictable environment. But the realists of crime control will settle for a derivative pragmatic version, sharing with the original a refusal to accept consciousness as a variable. As long as people behave themselves, something is achieved. The vision is quite happy to settle for sullen citizens performing their duties and not having insights (p. 124).

Behaviourism offers the possibility of a time-limited, highly focused, intervention which addresses behaviour which those with the power and authority to penalise it, want changed. It is a mechanistic approach which relegates questions of the meaning the behaviour has for the subject, or its social significance, to the category of unscientific speculation. The advantage of behaviourism is that in offering such quantifiable interventions to under-resourced agencies it also provides a rationale for a minimal intervention which can be 'sold' to the juvenile bench in terms of its scientific hard-headedness and political and theoretical neutrality. This approach requires of those who operate it an acceptance of the view of the offending behaviour taken by the police, the prosecutor and the magistrate. But outside the laboratory, in the real world, things are often more complicated than this.

Negative practice and the real world – the practitioner's dilemma

It had become evident by the end of the 1970s that whereas the apparatus of the juvenile justice system had expanded and there was, apparently, no limit on the amount the government was prepared to spend on law and order, services for young people in difficulty and in need had been decimated by cuts. The cruel irony was that this happened at a time when, arguably, young people in this country needed a comprehensive Youth Service more than they ever had before.

Workers confronted unprecedented levels of unemployment, an enormous growth in opiate addiction, rising levels of street-crime, and civil disorder on an unprecedented scale. This was also the period when it was at last recognised that many young people, young women, in particular, were the victims of sexual abuse by members of their own family. There was a similarly reluctant recognition that not only the opportunities, but also the mental health, and in some cases the lives, of black British young people were endangered by racism. Yet minimalism required workers to 'leave the kids alone' in order to concentrate upon their correctional programmes.

But news from across the Atlantic, when it was eventually heeded, began to cast doubt upon the myopia of minimalism. As Lloyd Ohlin (1979) noted: 'our research indicates that the network of relationships which youth maintain in the community have a crucial impact on their ability to stay out of trouble after their release. In fact, it seems clear that the total community experience of the youth before and after his correctional experience may overwhelm even the most constructive elements of the correctional programme' (p. 22).

Ohlin researched the Massachusetts Experiment, the most thoroughgoing attempt to decarcerate young offenders from correctional institutions ever attempted. It involved closing all state residential provision for young offenders and dispersing them into private and voluntary community-based provision. Massachusetts became something of a shibboleth for the minimalists but Ohlin's observations suggested that perhaps radical non-intervention was not enough and that if we wished to divert youngsters from danger as well as institutionalisation then we must address the worsening social world they inhabited.

It wasn't that the advocates of minimalism were wrong to criticise the theories which had informed social work interventions with young offenders or the unintended consequences of those interventions. It was that in their attempts to distance themselves from these theories and practices, rather than taking what they had to offer and moving on, they simply advocated their opposite. What was needed was a set of ideas and practices which were informed by both the achievements and the mistakes of the past and confronted the complexities of the present. This new paradigm is stil! in the making.

3

Towards a New Paradigm for Positive Practice

If the limitation of a minimalist approach was its myopic focus upon *social reaction* to individual young offenders, the limitation of 1960s-style 'welfarism' was its equally myopic concentration upon juvenile crime as pathological *social action*. A further limitation they shared was their reluctance to enter the real world. While minimalism found its spiritual habitat in the court, welfarism was most at home at a case conference. This refusal to address the relationship between juvenile crime, justice and broader social economic and political developments meant that both positions were victims of time and change. Being wedded to theories which only addressed one variable in the complex equation of crime, justice and victimisation, they were destined to be overtaken by events.

It was these events, intellectual, social and political, often emanating from quite unexpected quarters, which have supplied the raw material out of which a new paradigm for practice in juvenile justice might be constructed.

At last – an uprising

During the 1960s and early 1970s some workers with young people in trouble in the poorer sections of the inner-city were taxed by the question of whether, and to what extent, they should confront their clients with the political realities of their predicament (Robins and Cohen, 1978). This concern was prompted, in large part, by the recognition that in their attempts to offer compensatory experiences to socially deprived children and young people they might, in fact, be defusing an uprising.

When in 1981 this long-awaited uprising of youth eventually occurred the professional debate about youth and crime had already abandoned its concern with the politics of inequality in favour of a technical discussion between juvenile justice professionals about how the apparatus of justice might best be manipulated. During the turbulent spring of 1981 the centres of many major British cities were put to the torch in the wake of confrontations with the police. In the afterglow, those who had an eye for these things saw that unless juvenile justice professionals were prepared to acknowledge the political significance of these events and recognise that the issues of institutionalised racism and relative deprivation were at the core of the problem besetting the juvenile justice system in the late 1980s, they could, very quickly, become an irrelevance.

Racism and the rediscovery of aetiology

Unemployment, poor housing and poverty may have provided the fuel for the conflagration but it was, in almost all cases, conflict between the police and the Afro-Caribbean community which sparked it off. This gave added impetus to research into the relationship between black people and the criminal justice system.

This research revealed that black young people were policed more intensively than whites (Smith, 1983); that they were substantially less likely to be cautioned and diverted out of the juvenile justice system and, as a result, more likely to appear in court (Landau, 1981); that in court they were more likely to receive a custodial sentence (Taylor, 1982); that probation officers were less likely to recommend supervision in the community (Taylor, 1981; and De La Motta, 1984) and that social workers were less likely to recommend an alternative to custody (Pitts, 1988).

While it was probably true that disproportionately large numbers of black children and young people were involved in street crime, it was not street crime which was filling the jails and the CHEs with black adolescents (Pitts, 1986).

The overall population of children and young people in CHEs (the earlier Approved Schools) declined from the early 1970s and this was in large part a consequence of a decline in the use of the care order. Bottomley and Pease (1986) note that 'the proportionate use of these orders remained steady for the first half of the 1963–1973 period, with an increase in absolute numbers from 4000 to 7000, but in the following decade their use dropped dramatically to just over 2000'.

This overall decline masked the reality that an increasing proportion of the CHE population was composed of black children and young people. As early as 1971 Harris found that 32 per cent of girls and 52 per cent of boys in Approved Schools in London and the south-east were from ethnic minorities. In the mid-1980s black young people often constituted more than 60 per cent of the remand and assessment centre populations in the London area. These were boys and girls awaiting placement in CHEs. Meanwhile high-intensity IT day-care had relatively few black youngsters on its rolls (Pitts *et al.*, 1986). As we note in Chapter 5, some of the reasons for the disproportionate incarceration of black youngsters must be sought in the racist folklore about Afro-Caribbean child-rearing patterns which informs some social work practice. Research indicated that unemployment, homelessness and having previously spent some time in care were the factors which determined whether or not a young person received a custodial sentence in the crown court (Taylor, 1981; and Box and Hale, 1986). These factors are all indicators of poverty, a problem to which black children and young people in Britain are particularly prone.

Black young people in Britain occupy the most crowded accommodation and are as a consequence more prone to homelessness than their white counterparts. Because they tend to come from poor families with fewer resources they are also more likely to be received into local authority care (DHSS, 1986). While most young white people experience difficulty in the job market, unemployment levels amongst black people in the inner city often exceed 65 per cent (Guest, 1984). Magistrates and judges for their part have always dealt more severely with defendants who have 'no fixed abode' and 'no visible means of support'.

One of the consequences of this has been that in some institutions for young offenders black youngsters constitute a substantial minority, and in some cases, the majority of the inmates. Martin Kettle writing in 1982 noted that 'In April this year according to the Home Office 50% of the population of Ashford remand centre was black. Brixton (another remand prison) and Aylesbury prisons were between 25% and 35% black. So were Rochester, Dover and Hewell Grange borstals and Blantyre House detention centre' (p. 535). Something was happening which was far more complex and insidious than 'disparate bodies of professionals making the wrong decisions about the wrong children at the wrong time', and a classless and colour-blind minimalism was unable to explain it (Thorpe, 1980).

The discovery of the differential treatment of Afro-Caribbean young people in the juvenile justice system alerted us to the ways in which it was processing 'surplus' populations. The institutionalised racism experienced by black young people who fell foul of the law: echoed the institutionalised class discrimination which had always dogged the system. What was needed was a response which could be effective in countering institutionalised discrimination in the juvenile justice system and not just individual mistakes.

The strategy developed by the NACRO Juvenile Offenders Team involves intervention in the juvenile justice system of a town or borough at senior executive level. Working with the Chief Constable, the Chief Probation Officer, the Chief Education Officer, the Director of Social Services and the Senior Youth Officer they have tried to devise an integrated strategy for young offenders which is informed by their own research and spans 'social prevention' (see pp. 34–5 below), social compensation, diversion and reparation.

In the wake of the disorders of spring 1981 JOT became increasingly involved in developing anti-racist strategies in local juvenile justice systems. This involved setting targets for reductions in custodial sentencing of black children and young people, devising monitoring and gatekeeping mechanisms and establishing alternatives to custody geared to the needs of black young people.

JOT has devised an anti-racist strategy which, by asserting the need for preventive and compensatory measures and the expansion of opportunity, as well as diversion and reparation, responds to the evidence that black young people are offered far fewer educational and vocational opportunities than any other group in our society. As a result crime looms large in the narrow range of options available to them.

JOT-style systems interventions have added a sociological and a political dimension to minimalist modes of systems management. In doing this they have alerted us to the reality that an understanding of the origins of both juvenile crime, and discriminatory responses to it, can be translated into a 'systemic' solution to a 'systemic' problem.

The rediscovery of the victim

The research evidence on race, crime and justice indicated that in as much as black young people were co-opted to play the role of young offenders in a pre-existing social script constructed out of structural disadvantages, professional practices, ingrained prejudices and institutionalised power relationships, so were their victims. Lower-class white and black young people, it emerged, were not only more likely to be the perpetrators of juvenile crime but they were also more likely to be its victims as well. Young J. (1987) writes: 'if we look at the assault rate . . . we see that over 45 year old whites live in what amounts to a totally different universe with regards to crime than do younger people. Young, white females are, for example, twenty nine times more likely to be assaulted than those over 45, and thirty times more likely to be sexually attacked' (p. 10).

It was the recognition of the disproportionate criminal victimisation of the most vulnerable social groups, women, racial minorities and the poor which led to the demand for a police force accountable, and able to offer a reasonable level of social defence, to the victimised community.

Meanwhile Safe Neighbourhood projects were demonstrating that by a combination of community organisation, negotiation with the police, 'target hardening' and the development of informal social, educational and recreational interventions with young people on 'dangerous' housing estates, it was possible to make them safer. Bright and Petterson (1984) wrote that 'This experience suggests that on estates with a serious crime/vandalism/hooliganism problem that is thought to be caused by indigenous young people, a detached youth worker with a specific job brief should be deployed with responsibilities both for the welfare of the young people, and for reducing crime and deterring the harrassment of tenants' (p. 41).

Minimalism had found it convenient to assume, with labelling theory, that juvenile crime was no more than a relatively innocuous manifestation of working-class youth culture and as such best left alone. What the victimisation studies of the 1980s threw up was the reality that juvenile crime posed a serious threat to, and imposed a tax upon, the working-class community. As Lee and Young (1984) pointed out, it was precisely because the political left and liberal centre have been unwilling to come to grips with the reality of criminal victimisation that the issue has been annexed by the political right as a powerful and effective rallying cry. In such a political climate it was clear that if juvenile justice professionals wanted to have any impact on policy they had to have something to say about, and something to say to, the victims of juvenile crime.

Feminism and the Heysel Stadium riot

It was the emergence of feminist writing in the sphere of crime and justice which alerted us to the full extent of the victimisation of women and children by men and gave the impetus to victimisation studies, and eventually, some changes in child-care and policing policies.

At the same time some feminists working in the youth service and social work were attempting to develop an anti-sexist practice which opened up space for girls to develop their interests and potential. In this work girls were encouraged and supported to think about, and ask for, the things that they wanted and to question taken for granted assumptions about the roles they should play. This involved confronting boys about their taken for granted assumptions. This type of work, regarded by many, usually men, as somewhat esoteric, became highly relevant in 1985 when a large crowd of young British football supporters rioted and in the ensuing chaos 36 Italian fans were killed.

When the culprits were extradited to Belgium in 1987 the *Sun* demanded that 'our lads' should be brought back 'home' in a front-page feature which scarcely concealed the belief that their behaviour was in some way mitigated because the victims were 'foreigners'. In a similar vein, a British fan involved in the violence surrounding the European Cup match in Stuttgart in 1988 said in a radio interview: 'we know Margaret Thatcher and the Government and everybody at home supports us, but they're not allowed to say so, are they?' Other commentators, usually male, from across the whole political spectrum, were simply stunned and perplexed by the phenomenon. But many women were not, knowing from their own experience that the young man on the radio was right and that there was a great deal of support for this type of behaviour. They knew that under the wrong circumstances, the normal xenophobic and homophobic, socialisation of white British men could lead them into apparently inexplicable violence (Gregory, 1986).

It was the horror of the spectacle of innocent bystanders being crushed to death which made the Heysel Stadium riot the focus for the discussion about the relationship between football and violence. Given the episodic nature of this violence and the fact that it never involved the girls and women who also attended football matches, the discussion moved quite rapidly to the question of male violence in general.

Male violence to women, children and other men is rife and we are only just beginning to gauge its true dimensions (Jones, 1986). But as feminist theorists and practitioners in juvenile justice have shown, widespread male violence is not simply a problem of too many violent men.

In our society men and women are given rigid injunctions about how they should play their gender roles. These 'scripts' are modified by culture and subculture and provide the repertoire of social meanings, and prescriptions for action, upon which they draw in their attempts to establish and maintain an identity. Men can and do make choices about how they play their role. When, however, they are subjected to pressure, or denied the means to demonstrate their social value they will often fall back upon shared archetypes of a crude and violent 'maleness' which is their shared legacy of normal male socialisation.

If the trouble with girls was that as a result of their socialisation they had learnt to bury their aggression and anger and subordinate their own needs for care, dependency and gratification to the needs of others, the trouble with boys was that they hadn't (Eichenbaum and Orbach, 1983). The problem for both was to transcend the partiality of their socialisation in order to become whole people.

This threw a new light upon the 'boys' work', pioneered by feminists, suggesting that it might offer a fruitful mode of intervention with boys who were expressing this maleness, or their anxieties about it, through violent or destructive behaviour. It was also clear that many of the responses to young offenders, with their emphasis on toughness, 'challenge' and discipline actually colluded with the archetype and worsened the problem to which they were the intended solution.

This was an important insight. If male violence was, in large part, about the difficulties men experienced in being valued as people, perhaps the task was not to equip them with the social skills to live up to a set of highly problematic social expectations but to help them to gain sufficient critical distance on these expectations in order to explore what was actually valuable about them.

This analysis posed a serious challenge to most of the traditional practices in the juvenile justice system which are dominated by male (ocentric) assumptions about what constitutes a problem and what constitutes a reasonable male solution to it. It also offered a potentially fruitful way of understanding and working with the problems of male anxiety, violence and destructiveness.

Heroin

The import, repackaging and distribution of heroin has been one of the few growth industries in Britain in the 1980s. Geoffrey Pearson (1987) writes: 'By the mid-1980s, the official number of heroin addicts had increased alarmingly by British standards to more than twelve thousand. It is a fair guess that the actual number of heroin users in Britain by this time was well in excess of 50,000, and possibly somewhere between 60,000 and 80,000' (p. 3).

In the abuse of heroin we find an offence in which, at street-level at least, the perpetrator is usually the victim as well. As such the small-scale abuse of the drug might well be decriminalised. For minimalism the argument for decriminalisation has invariably been part and parcel of the argument for non-intervention. In this context heroin abuse has offered an instructive example of the problems of minimal, or non-intervention.

Attempts to develop tightly-focused 'treatment' responses to heroin abuse have sometimes foundered because they have been based upon the assumption that heroin abuse is essentially a problem of availability and susceptibility in which groups or individuals with a heightened vulnerability to addiction become embroiled with a supplier. A South London detached youth work project designed to make contact with users and addicts ground to a halt because the users had not separated themselves off into a separate subculture but continued to associate with non-users. The project moved instead to a strategy of offering local professional and voluntary workers with young people, information about drugs and support in working with young people who were dependent on them. Indeed Pearson (1987) found that drug abuse tended to infuse whole neighbourhoods as a collective solution to a shared problem: 'Even within a town or city with a major problem, it will tend to be concentrated in certain neighbourhoods and virtually unknown in others. Moreover where the problem has tended to gather together in dense pockets within our towns and cities, this will usually be in neighbourhoods which are the worse affected by unemployment and wretched housing' (pp. 3–4).

Pearson argues, as do many workers in the field, that the problem of heroin abuse cannot be abstracted from the problems afflicting the neighbourhood in which the heroin abuser lives: 'In that sense the new heroin problem is not just an individual problem. It is also a collective responsibility, whereby the possibilities for people to lead meaningful and rewarding lives and fashion effective identities in these rundown working-class neighbourhoods of so many of our towns and cities must be rebuilt. It will be a long climb' (pp. 190–1).

Heroin abuse emerges in Pearson's analysis not as a piece of irrational behaviour to which a 'naturally' vulnerable individual 'junkie' is drawn, like an iron filing to a magnet. This is no individual abberation but a moment in an enormously complex set of international business transactions. Heroin is the perfect drug for the unemployed. A habit structures peoples lives, it gives them a reason to get out of bed in the morning, or the evening.

Procuring the price of a 'bag', scoring the stuff and then taking it, make for a busy life, while the effect at least initially offers a euphoric holiday from the grinding tedium of not enough money and nowhere to go. An examination of the contours of contemporary heroin abuse alerts us to the dangers of individualising problems experienced by individuals.

The emergence of consumerism

The 1980s saw the growth of consumerism among groups of young people who had previously been denied a public hearing. Developed initially by children's rights activists and other interested adults the Who Cares organisation came of age in the 1980s as the National Association of Young People In Care (NAYPIC) which in turn spawned Black and In Care.

These groups have articulated the needs of children and young people in local authority care and translated these needs into a charter of rights which local NAYPIC groups use as a basis for negotiation with local authorities. They have focused attention on the need for young people to be adequately prepared for independent living when they leave residential care, adequately financed to do so and adequately supported when they have done so. While the focus of the consumer groups is not upon young people who offend, it is quite clear that a substantial section of the long-term inmates of young offender institutions and prisons are people who have made an unsuccessful transition from residential care to independent living. The experience of long-term residential care can be socially disabling. As well as a heightened vulnerability to imprisonment, young people who have spent lengthy periods in residential care are over-represented in the populations of psychiatric institutions, among prostitutes, male and female, among drug addicts and among the victims of violent assaults and murder (Millham, 1986).

These consumers of social welfare have advanced the 'rights versus needs' debate considerably (Carlen, 1983). They have attempted to build rights and safeguards for children and young people into local authority procedures and campaigned for the right of youngsters in care to have a say in decisions which affect their lives.

One of the rights upon which they have insisted is the right to good, consistent and reliable social work intervention in their lives to help them with their needs and problems. In doing this they have avoided both the rampant 'needology' of welfarism and the arid legalism of the liberal justice lobby. We learn two things from this. First, polarisation is usually simplistic and tends to miss the point. Second, children and young people are often much more sensible and objective than highly educated adults with an axe to grind.

The European experience

As we have seen, many of the theories we use to account for deviant behaviour, and many of our responses to it, are imported from the USA. This has been a fruitful transaction but it has sometimes led us to perpetuate the assumption that what happens in the USA today will happen in Britain tomorrow. Partly because of the accessibility of the American experience through shared language and partly because of the 'special relationship' we have tended not to consider, or learn from, experiences in societies which are, in fact, more similar to our own. In the 1980s, as the reality of the Common Market percolated popular consciousness, juvenile justice professionals began to look to Europe, and found there an antidote to the unrelenting pessimism which had afflicted Anglo-American theory and practice in recent years (Klein, 1984).

The contrast between Britain and other European countries was brought home to me during a visit to The Netherlands with a party of student social workers in 1983. Having spent a week in discussions and visits, courtesy of the Ministry of Justice, we were impressed by the progressiveness and liberality of the Dutch system. In a burst of unreflective generosity a student invited our hosts to Britain to study our system. One of them, a senior administrator in the Dutch prison system, smiled and replied: 'thank you very much, but we are penologists not historians, perhaps we could go sightseeing instead.'

In recent years events in the Italian and French juvenile justice systems have offered tantalising examples of what might be done in changed political circumstances.

Italy

In June 1988 there were two young men serving custodial sentences in the youth prison in Bologna in Italy. The Bologna Youth Prison serves the province of Emilia Romagna which has a population of approximately 15 million people. Bologna is a small town with a progressive local authority, but in the northern industrial cities of Turin and Milan we witness a similar reluctance to imprison juveniles. Lemert (1986) notes that at each stage in the Italian juvenile justice process, either by formal or informal means, agents of the system appear to work hard to divert youngsters out of it. In drawing a comparison between Italy and California USA, he notes: 'Over fourteen times as many arrests of minors were made in California as in Italy in 1980. When a correction is made to account for differences in population of the two places the number rises to twenty-eight times as many arrests in California as in Italy.' Of the proportion of those arrested who eventually came to court he writes: 'Of course allowances must be made for the fact that California police screen out many cases. . . . However this still amounts to somewhat over fourteen times as many court referrals in California as in all Italy in 1980' (p. 530).

This low-key approach to juvenile crime in Italy is attributable in part to the central importance attributed to the family as a source of social control and the willingness of agents of the system to let the family deal with problems of petty crime. Linked closely to this is the widespread view that the juvenile court, which was introduced in 1934 by Mussolini, does not constitute an appropriate or useful response to problems of juvenile offending. Beyond this however lies the fact that in Italy, and in many other European countries, juvenile crime does not carry the same symbolic and political significance that it does in Britain and the USA.

In Italy in recent times social anxiety has focused on terrorism, Mafia crime and the related problem of drug abuse amongst 20 to 30 year olds and this has eclipsed police and public interest in the offences of minors. In Italy juvenile crime is, to all intents and purposes, depoliticised. One of the many things that we can learn from Italy is that depolitisation, the deflection of public, media and political concern onto more appropriate phenomena and its concomitant, political indifference, can sometimes clear the 'ideological space' in which quiet but effective reform can occur.

France

In response to violent disturbances in the ghetto suburbs of Lyons and Marseilles in 1981, and fearing that the situation might assume the crisis proportions it had in Britain, the Mitterrand government established an interdepartmental commission and two committees of enquiry to devise a long-term response to the problem. It also immediately introduced a programme of summer camps and activities, known as the *étés-jeunes*. These programmes of sporting, educational, vocational and cultural activities were developed with, and in large part directed by, the children and young people of the ghettos. In 1983, its second year of operation, 100 000 children and young people participated in the programme. The French initiative exhumed and breathed new life into the idea of prevention and many thousands of socially disadvantaged young people were attracted to it. Yet the question of whether the programmes actually prevented crime remained. King (1987) observed that: 'A simple answer would be that the French criminal statistics indicate a decline over the last two years in the type of offence likely to be committed by young people, such as criminal damage, theft, taking cars and minor assaults. As a whole, crime in France has fallen by 10.5% during this period with a fall of over 8% between 1985 and 1986' (p. 5).

As a result of the commission and the enquiries initiated in 1981 a structure of delinquency prevention councils was created. At town level they are chaired by the mayor and maintain links with local youth groups. At national level the mayors represent their towns on the Conseil National de Prevention de la Delinquence which is chaired by the Prime Minister. These committees are now a permanent feature of French political life and 'social prevention' is a permanent aspect of French social provision.

What we learn from France is that escalating levels of crime and civil disorder are not an inevitable corollary of economic recession if the political will exists to offer compensatory experiences to, and to create new opportunities for, those youngsters who bear the brunt of the recession. We might also note that social prevention was made more politically viable and less likely to serve as a 'net-widening' mechanism because:

> An essential feature in the success of the French initiative has been the political consensus that what was needed was a co-operative, non-repressive approach to youth crime. It should be remembered that France has never had detention centres or Borstals. The nearest equivalent, the *Centres Fermés* ceased to exist after 1978 after social workers employed by the Ministry of Justice had refused to participate in the incarceration of children. Short of locking large numbers of adolescents in adult prisons, therefore, the option of using the courts and penal establishments to control youth violence did not exist for the French. Some alternative to repression had to be found' (King, 1987, p. 3).

It is ironical to reflect that in Britain, where we lock-up a higher proportion of our young offenders than any other European country apart from Turkey, violent crime and civil disorder continued to grow unabated throughout the decade.

It seems that political indifference, as was the case in Italy, and political commitment, as was the case in France, can both be mobilised to promote reform. This has led people involved in juvenile justice in Britain to think about strategies which might be employed to alter the ideological climate in a way that would promote juvenile justice reform.

Towards a new paradigm

A consideration of the past and an appreciation of the problems of the present do not throw up a fully formed prescription for future action and nor should they. It is always tempting to fall into the '20/20 hindsight' fallacy in which we assume that an appreciation of the limitations of previous orthodoxies will enable us to perfect a new one. Social work abounds with orthodoxies and the factionalism which they generate, and the losers are invariably the clients. What we need instead are some principles which will assist us in understanding, and in intervening constructively with, young offenders.

Understanding young offenders

The perspective developed in this book is that offending is a way, albeit often inadequate and self-defeating, of solving problems. It follows from this that in our attempt to understand the motivation of young offenders we should try to understand the origins of the problems to which their offending is an attempted solution.

Feminism has alerted us to the necessity of understanding male violence simultaneously at the levels of *Structure*, *Culture* and *Biography*. Social and cultural forces have prescribed the 'solutions' which men believe are, available to them and this has legitimised violent behaviour and proscribed certain non-violent options. Similarly, when we consider the disproportionate involvement of black children and young people in crimes of poverty it is clear that we cannot understand a particular piece of offending behaviour without considering the social and cultural forces which have shaped the offender's *Consciousness* of the world they inhabit and how they are valued in it. Neither can we abstract the offender or the offence from their material circumstances and the real, legitimate and illegitimate, opportunities available to them in their pursuit of a solution to the experience of relative deprivation.

Every offence has a *Past* in terms of the way the offenders have come to see themselves in the world, and the material reality of that world; a *Present* in which beliefs, feelings, wants and needs are operationalised in (illegal) action and to which a control apparatus responds; and a *Future* in which the social reaction which the action has evoked may change both the offenders' identity, by recasting them as deviants, and the opportunities available to them. Understanding young offenders involves the attempt to understand the past, present and the future of the offence.

Intervening with young offenders

James Q. Wilson (1975), as we have noted, believed that no practical purpose could be served by identifying the ultimate origins of a deviant act and this was a belief he shared with other minimalists.

Pearson's (1988) analysis of the problem of heroin abuse locates it as a solution to the problem of earning a living, for the people who grow it and a solution to the problem of not earning a living for the people who use it. For both, the problem is a consequence of the roles they play, or are prevented from playing, in the social and economic system.

Some black, unemployed, homeless youngsters trapped in the unemployment ghetto at the bottom of the social structure seek a solution in a spate of burglaries but quickly find themselves confronting a juvenile justice system which will treat them more harshly because they are black, unemployed and homeless.

In each case we find people whose attempts to devise a solution to their relative powerlessness in one system has put them at the mercy of another system which holds the potential to do them even greater harm. The problem concerns the roles these people are allowed to play and the effect this has on the relationships which they will be able to maintain in the systems of which they are a part. Wilson presents us with the essential criminal constrained by ultimate causes and destined to cut a deviant swathe through the world. The offender presented here, by contrast, is a person who lacks bargaining power and, as a consequence, a reasonable repertoire of status-conferring roles to play in the world.

If we view the problem systemically in this way, focusing on the transactions between actors within the system and not simply the 'essential' qualities of the deviant individual, we are presented with four different potential areas of intervention. There is the social and economic system which bears upon the young offender and offers, or withholds opportunity from them, the juvenile justice system which compounds or ameliorates the problems experienced by the offender; their immediate social mileau; which comprises their family, friends and other people who exert influence upon, or control over, them and finally the offender themselves with their skills abilities feelings, beliefs and desires.

The notion of ultimate causes is a red herring. Crime and deviance, like social conformity are products of transactions within and between social systems. We search not simply for the ultimate causes of the problem but for effective points of intervention in the systems of which the client is part, to help devise alternative solutions. This is what the Mitterrand government was doing when it pioneered its social prevention schemes, and what JOT was doing when it gathered together groups of chief executives in the welfare and justice bureaucracies in British cities and boroughs.

The problem with the strategies for change adopted by early systems management initiatives and the liberal justice lobby was that they addressed the administration of the system and ignored the political and face-to-face levels. The problem with social work strategies developed in the wake of the 1969 CYPA was that they addressed the face-to-face level but ignored the administrative and political levels. The problem with the prescriptions for change offered by sections of the left in the 1970s was that, in their insistence that after the revolution both the state and crime would wither away, they ignored the administrative and face-to-face levels.

A new paradigm, if it were to be informed by the past, would insist that in a sensible world we should devise interventions which operated simultaneously at *Political*, *Administrative* and *Face-to-Face* levels. What is clear though is that work at a political level which attempts, for example, to modify the law or persuade councillors of the need for a particular kind of provision will take a long time and if successful will benefit tomorrow's clients but not today's. So another principle which should inform our interventions is that having identified the appropriate levels of intervention we should establish whether our objectives can be achieved in the *short*, *medium* or *long* term.

Thus far progressives in juvenile justice in Britain have found it convenient to ignore the victim. Victimisation studies confront us with the reality that the victims of juvenile crime are frequently as deprived and vulnerable as the perpetrators. In the light of recent victimisation studies and, a changed political climate, we can no longer expect to be taken seriously by politicians or their constituents unless our paradigm recognises the predicament of the victim and offers an effective response to *Victimisation*.

4

The Juvenile Justice System

The term Juvenile Justice System, when it is used in this book, refers to the laws, professional practices and institutions created to respond to children and young people aged 10 to 17 years in England and Wales who are suspected, or found guilty of, committing a criminal offence. It is a system which is beset with problems and contradictions.

The 'treatment' oriented provisions of the 1969 C&YP Act were simply grafted onto a range of sentencing options which included the punitive DCs and Borstals. The 1982 CJ Act, as we have already noted, complicated things further by introducing additional 'justice' oriented measures.

The system has grown by a process of accretion in which new philosophies or symbols of political grit have been superimposed upon the existing system to form yet another stratum. We are left, as a result, with a juvenile justice system dogged by conflicting theories and philosophies concerning the nature of the problem and the nature of the solution.

The conflicts in the system have become institutionalised over time and are expressed in the divergent objectives and values of its agents and agencies. This theoretically unworkable situation works in practice, either because the different agents and agencies in the system reach some form of accommodation or compromise, or because they each decide to go their own way, Farrington D. (1984) argues that 'A plausible interpretation of the figures is that after the 1969 Act was introduced in 1971 the magistrates were avoiding sentences for which social workers were responsible. This led to an increase in the more lenient sentences (discharges and fines), and also in the more severe institutional sentences' (pp.

88–9). While a national picture of this type accurately reflects overall developments, it does not throw light upon the highly variable practices of the multiplicity of local juvenile justice systems.

The local juvenile justice system

So far we have referred to the 'juvenile justice system' as if it were a national institution which operated in a uniform way dispensing uniform justice throughout the land. The juvenile justice system of England and Wales is in fact composed of a multiplicity of local juvenile justice systems which are characterised by idiosyncracy rather than uniformity. Indeed, what happens to a child or young person in the system will be shaped as much by the area in which he or she commits the offence as its seriousness. The differences between local juvenile justice systems will be determined in large part by the formal and informal relationships which are established between the agencies and agents which constitute the structure of the system and the ways in which they chose to use their powers.

Systems are characterised by interdependence and this means that power, rather than being concentrated in one place, is dispersed throughout the system. Each actor within the system needs the others and so, in varying degrees, power is bestowed upon them all. Capra (1982) notes that: 'Systems theory looks at the world in terms of the inter-relatedness and interdependence of all phenomena. . . . An integrated whole whose properties cannot be reduced to those of its parts is called a system (p. 26).

It is this 'inter-relatedness and inter-dependence' which offers the key to our interventions. A systemic view alerts us to the reality that, when agents and agencies within a system effect choices about whether, and how, to use their power, those choices will have consequences for the whole system. These choices will affect the youngster's life in significant ways and it follows that if we are to work in the interests of the young offender it will often be these relationships and these choices which will constitute the target for our interventions and the exercise of our power. Systems can be sites of conflict, consensus, or negotiation. What they become will be determined by the ways in which the actors within them choose to use their power.

Induction and diversion

Truancy brings more children and young people into the juvenile justice system than any other offence. It is a 'status offence' which can only be committed by children and young people between the ages of 5 and 16. Civil libertarians have drawn attention to the irony that schooling is the only social service which we can be locked up for not using. While the responsibilities of the Educational Welfare Service (EWS) include counselling, assessments for free school meals and uniforms and assessments of parental contributions to boarding school fees, it is as an agency responsible for the surveillance and control of truancy that it inducts children and young people into the juvenile justice system.

Persistent truancy is regarded in many juvenile courts as more serious than petty offending. As a result most of the young people despatched to CHEs are truants who have committed petty offences rather than serious juvenile criminals with a tendency to stay away from school (Thorpe, 1980). The development in the mid-1970s of off-site units for 'difficult' and truanting pupils, the controversial involvement of Intermediate Treatment with truanting children, of which more later, and early attempts at systems management were, to a greater or lesser extent, an attempt to stem this exodus to the CHEs.

The EWS, having issued a number of warnings and visited the child and the family, will initiate legal proceedings under the 1944 Education Act or the 1969 CYPA. These proceedings may well lead to magistrates deferring their decision pending the outcome of a 'trial attendance' at school. If the attendance is satisfactory then the case will usually be dismissed. If it is not, then the parents will be prosecuted under the 1944 Act or the child will be made the subject of a care or supervision order under the 1969 Act.

This process can sometimes be a source of antagonism between the social workers employed by the EWS and those employed by the local authority. Local authority social workers argue that the EWS, having used the prosecution as a sign that they mean business, leave them 'to do the business'. Educational welfare officers for their part cite the confused bureaucratic and legal paraphernalia which surrounds their job and results in them having to transfer their cases to social workers in another agency who lack expertise in, and give a low priority to, social problems in the school.

These difficulties notwithstanding, educational welfare officers working in conjunction with the school, the youngster, the local authority social worker and the family are often able to devise alternatives to legal intervention which make it possible to divert the truanting pupil away from the juvenile justice system. Their role may involve advocacy and negotiation between each of the parties and the identification of alternative educational settings in which the erstwhile truant will be able to fulfil his or her social obligation to get an education. It is for these reasons that educational welfare officers have a key role to play on the inter-agency panels discussed below. The other route into the juvenile justice system is via the police station.

Most young offenders enter the juvenile justice system when they are apprehended by the police. At the police station the station officer will decide whether the young person's case should be referred to the Crown Prosecution Service or whether it can be dealt with by the Youth and Community Bureau which has the power to take 'no further action' (NFA) or formally 'caution' the young offender. This is one of the points where discrepancies between local juvenile justice systems is very evident. Cautioning practices vary widely from area to area. In 1986, whereas the Northamptonshire police cautioned 85 per cent of the boys and 95 per cent of the girls it apprehended, the figures for Staffordshire were 43 per cent and 88 per cent respectively. The extent to which cautioning is used to divert youngsters out of a local system tends to be determined by the degree of inter-agency consultation which takes place at the point of arrest. Many police forces take part in, or arrange to receive recommendations from, panels of professionals working with young people.

> These typically include representatives from the police, probation service, education, social services and education welfare. Occasionally, others such as the youth service and community groups may be represented on the panel. Ideally the panel members work as a team and make joint decisions and recommendations. However the general practice is for the panel to make recommendations to the police who hold final responsibility for decision-making. It should also be recognised and accepted that decision-making can be difficult. This is because the different agencies involved have different roles and different primary responsibilities in respect of young people (NACRO, 1987, p. 5).

In some areas where effective panels have been established and close co-operation exists between the agencies, the proportion of cases which actually enter the court has been dramatically reduced. This has led some commentators to announce, somewhat prematurely, the advent of the 'custody-free zone' and to imply that if only workers in other areas were to adopt the model then they too could effect similarly dramatic changes in their own local juvenile justice systems.

This is, however, an illustration of how difficult, indeed dangerous, it is to assume that a practice which works well in one area can be exported lock, stock and barrel into another. The areas where custody-free zones have been declared are either small towns or semi-rural districts in which the numbers of those entering custody are very small. The very effective initiative mounted by the Rainer Foundation, and supported by the police and the juvenile bench in Basingstoke, reduced the number of youngsters entering the prison system from 18 in 1980 to two in 1983. This was a proportionate reduction of 900 per cent and if this effect could be replicated throughout England and Wales it would bring about profound changes in the national juvenile justice system.

If we contrast Basingstoke with the London Borough of Lambeth during the same period we see that, far from youngsters being diverted out of the system, by the differential use of 'stop and search' procedures, criminal attempts/SUS prosecutions, and cautioning in relation to black young people, the police were in fact drawing increasing numbers of them into it (Smith, 1983; Demuth, 1978; and Landau, 1981). Stevens and Willis (1979), noting that black young people were 14 and 15 times respectively more likely to be arrested for the offences of 'other violent theft' and 'being a suspected person' (SUS), commented: 'These ratios are so much higher than might be expected that they give rise to the question whether arrest rates are accurate indicators of relative black and white involvement in crime and if not whether some of the difference may be accounted for by the possibility that the suspicions of policemen bear disproportionatley on blacks' (p. 33).

Basingstoke and Lambeth are not simply in different leagues in the same game. The policing role in Lambeth is deeply imbued with concerns about the maintenance of public order and the need to exert maximum surveillance and control over what is perceived to be a highly volatile population. Black young people for their part often share the view held in other sections of the black community that the police is a racist force which usually works against their interests (Lee and Young, 1984).

In these circumstances any intervention with the agents of the local juvenile justice system in Lambeth may well need to address not just decisions about a particular young person, but about policing strategies in particular neighbourhoods and relationships between an entire community and its police force. As a result the inter-agency panel may not be the forum in which significant change can occur and the professional workers may concentrate their efforts instead upon the local police liaison or police accountability group. In Basingstoke change in the juvenile justice system was effected primarily at the administrative level. In Lambeth it appears that effective administrative change has only been possible in the wake of political change.

As we have noted, through the use of cautioning and NFA decisions it has been possible to limit, and in some cases reduce substantially, the numbers of children and young people, appearing before magistrates in the juvenile court. This endeavour, known in the USA as 'front end' diversion, should result in only the most serious cases coming before the court. As we have also noted, however, partly because of the different types of offences in which black young people are involved, but largely as a result of the differential policing of black and white citizens, a higher proportion of less serious black young offenders enter the juvenile court (Martin, 1985; Tipler, 1985). In areas where inter-agency panels do not exist the onus is on the social workers to act as advocates for their clients when they are arrested.

In court

In the 1980s the number of children and young people entering the juvenile court, as well as the number receiving a custodial sentence once there, declined. Whereas in 1981 7700 juveniles were given custodial sentences, by 1987 this figure had dwindled to 4000. This is attributable, in varying degrees, to the success of the diversionary initiatives of the type pioneered by JOT, the development of alternatives to custody and a reduction in the numbers of youngsters in the age group. However, this overall reduction obscures the reality that the 1980s also witnessed a substantial increase in the confinement of black young people in child-care and penal institutions. While we have to recognise that part of this increase was attributable to the high proportion of children and young people in the Afro-Caribbean population, it is quite clear that the differential sentencing of black and white children and young people was a major cause (Taylor, 1982; Berry, 1984). This has led both practitioners and governments to consider how the behaviour of judges and magistrates might be influenced. As we shall see, however, in the juvenile court the magistrate enjoys considerable power and autonomy.

The juvenile court is usually presided over by three lay magistrates, one of whom acts as chairperson. Sometimes, usually in large cities, a stipendiary magistrate who is a legally trained professional may also hear juvenile cases alone.

Magistrates can impose a broad range of penalties. At the bottom end of the tariff are the absolute discharge, conditional discharge, which usually requires youngsters to refrain from the behaviour which has brought them to court, and small fines. If the magistrate believes that a young person needs further help, guidance or surveillance they may make a supervision order. They will then expect a social worker to maintain regular contact with the young offender and 'advise, assist and befriend' them. A supervision order with an IT requirement allows the supervisor greater discretion in that he or she may require a young offender to participate in social, recreational or therapeutic activities.

Should the magistrate desire a more intensive form of intervention, he or she may make a supervision order with a specified activity order (SAO). In this case the young person may be required to undertake, or refrain from, activities specified by a magistrate and supervised by a social worker. A similarly 'tough' penalty available to the courts is the attendance centre order. The offender may be required to attend the centre on Saturday afternoons for a specified number of hours, up to a maximum of 24, to undertake drill, first-aid, crafts and other, similar, activities.

Probably the most intrusive penalty a court can impose upon a young offender this side of incarceration, is the community service order. This sentence, which can only be imposed on people over the age of 16, requires them to work for up to 120 hours on a community project under the supervision of a Community Service

Supervisor. Should youngsters not comply with the order, then, as is the case with the IT requirement and the SAO, the social worker is required to return them to court. Here the social worker or probation officer brings the prosecution and offers evidence of the youngster's breach of his or her order.

The most serious penalties involve removing a youngster from home. The magistrate can make a care order under the offence condition of the 1969 C&YP Act which transfers parental rights to the local authority. This responsibility is, to all intents and purposes, discharged by the social worker, who will decide whether, and if so when, a young offender should be placed in a Community Home (with Education) (CHE). Should youngsters re-offend while subject to this type of care order the court may impose a 'charge and control' condition which requires the local authority to place young offenders away from their own homes.

At the time of writing it seems likely that the Children Act, due to be implemented in 1991, will replace the care order in juvenile criminal proceedings with a new type of supervision order. Like the charge and control condition, this order may be couched in the negative, specifying only where a child or young person should not live rather than directing him or her to a particular type of residential facility.

The ultimate sanction a juvenile court can impose on young offenders over the age of 14 is imprisonment in a young offender institution. If such a sentence is imposed the young person's social worker or probation officer has a statutory responsibility to maintain contact for the duration of the sentence and the period of post-release licence which follows it.

The institution of the magistracy dates back to feudal times and was brought into being in an attempt to exert some control over drunkenness and crime amongst young people. The continuance of this ancient institution into the modern world is justified on the grounds that it offers an invaluable repository of lay common sense. It is argued that the attitudes and beliefs of lay magistrates will be more akin to those of the 'man in the street' than those of lawyers and judges, recruited largely from the upper middle classes. It is said that a magistracy composed of people from different social backgrounds with differing views, attitudes, and opinions will reflect the range of moral and social attitudes held in the wider society. The magistracy is presented as an important democratising and humanising element in the justice system.

Research has cast doubt upon the extent to which magistrates are representative of the wider society. Despite some changes in the 1980s the social make-up of the bench remains slanted in favour of the propertied, prosperous, well-educated and white while the defendants tend to be propertyless, poor, badly-educated and disproportionately black. The diversity of views held by magistrates may make them representative as a body but will tend to make them unrepresentative as individuals and it is as individuals that they hear cases. As a result penalties imposed upon both adults and juveniles vary widely from court to court and from area to area reflecting the idiosyncracies of particular courts or individual magistrates rather than what the public might feel is just (Burney, 1979; King and May, 1985).

These idiosyncracies mean that the relationship which exists between magistrates and social workers in any particular local juvenile justice system will be the subject of an ongoing negotiation. Some magistrates conceive of their major task as balancing the competing claims of deterrence, punishment, atonement and social protection and when they seek advice about sentencing they tend to seek it from the Clerk of the Court. The Clerk is the legally trained professional who is permanently attached to the court and serves as its adviser. Many social workers feel that Clerks should confine themselves to the clarification of points of law and not participate actively in decisions about sentences as happens in some courts (Burney, 1984). The Clerk may not be the power behind the throne but he or she is certainly the power beside the bench. Magistrates come and go but 'Clerks' abide and in doing so make a deep impression upon the way that 'their' court operates. Whether a juvenile court is tough or lenient is usually determined by the sentencing advice given to magistrates by the Clerk of the court. Clerks are there, notionally at least, to ensure consistency between magistrates and proportionality in sentencing. Although they are often unsuccessful in both of these endeavours it is remarkable how each juvenile court takes on a clearly identifiable persona.

The consistency of sentencing which is achieved tends to be internal to particular courts. Different juvenile courts operate substantially different sentencing tariffs. The sentencing options which are used, and the seriousness with which particular kinds of behaviour, like truancy, are viewed by a particular court are often shaped to a significant degree by the influence of the Clerk.

Welfare professionals in the juvenile justice system have sometimes attempted to devise ways of making a greater impact upon sentencing in situations where decisions made by a bench are either consistently idiosyncratic or discriminatory. Denied the opportunity to enact the roles of expert witness and sentencing adviser which are the base from which they usually exert their influence, they have attempted to devise alternative strategies which involve intervention at political and administrative levels.

In one area in South London workers monitored the sentences imposed by magistrates in terms of the racial origins of defendants, their previous convictions, the seriousness of the offence, and their home and employment circumstances. An analysis of this material revealed that black young men were being sentenced more harshly than other groups. These findings were then presented at one of their regular meetings with magistrates and the clerk where they were greeted with a mixture of shock, denial and genuine concern. In this way the workers were able to mobilise the concern of many of the magistrates in a way which would have been impossible if they had confined themselves to their more traditional role of offering opinions and recommendations about particular cases. As a result of their intervention sentencing patterns were changed.

There are many similar examples of magistrates working alongside social workers to ensure a fairer deal for the client. In some areas diversionary programmes and alternatives to custody have been brought into being as a result of the efforts of magistrates and Clerks of the court. As with other professional groups who operate in other areas of the juvenile justice system, it is dangerous to generalise about magistrates and Clerks. This said, however, it has to be acknowledged that juvenile court magistrates and Clerks have often constituted a formidable barrier to progress and reform (Box and Hale, 1986).

The sentencing tariff

The 'inputs' of the juvenile justice system are the children and young people who are apprehended by the police or whose persistent truancy leads to an official intervention by an education welfare officer. One of its main 'outputs' are the 'disposals', the decisions or sentences, imposed by the juvenile court. The range of disposals available to the court constitutes the tariff. The tariff is the expression *par excellence* of the ideological and theoretical conflicts which dog the system and conspire to propel a young offender through a bewildering variety of responses to ostensibly similar behaviour, as the following fairytale illustrates.

Nimrod's system career

At the age of 13 Nimrod becomes so interested in motor cars that he begins to spend time, when he should be at school, wandering the streets trying to find one he can get into. The police apprehend him and on the first three occasions he is 'cautioned'. On the fourth the police agree to caution him only if he agrees to attend a 'preventive' IT group. At the group he plays board games, makes models and cooks rock cakes.

Nonetheless Nimrod does it again and the police decide that this time they must prosecute. In court he is fined £5. The magistrate notes that he attends a 'preventive' IT project in his neighbourhood and expresses regret that thus far it has not apparently prevented very much.

Undaunted, Nimrod persists in his automotive misdemeanours and at his next appearance the court, believing that some more powerful form of intervention is required, the magistrate makes Nimrod the subject of a supervision order. The supervising social worker attempts to identify, and work with, the psycho-social family disfunction which is at the root of Nimrod's delinquency but the family lacks insight and fails to co-operate with the therapy.

Nimrod steals another car and when he appears in court his social worker asks whether, rather than sending Nimrod into care or custody, the magistrate would append an IT requirement to the existing supervision order so that Nimrod can participate in an alternative to custody where he would pursue the correctional curriculum.

When Nimrod reappears in court charged with five further offences he is sentenced to the brisk regime of an Attendance Centre, where he learns to march, say 'sir' to the police officers who staff the centre and give the 'kiss of life' to an expired rubber humanoid. The magistrate hopes that the experience will instill the discipline which is so clearly lacking in Nimrod's life. Alas, Nimrod's new-found discipline merely leads him to steal cars on a regular, rather than a sporadic, basis and as a result the police quickly get a fix on him and take him back to court. The magistrate is perplexed. Clearly something is seriously wrong and something serious has to be done about it; but what?

The court imposes a care order. The social worker returns and consigns Nimrod to a CHE which operates as a therapeutic community. There, he spends his days in unstructured groups confronting and being confronted by, the real needs he is trying to satisfy through his criminal behaviour. Eventually the pressure becomes too great. Nimrod steals the principal's car and absconds. He is eventually captured after a 100 mph chase along the M4. In court he is sentenced to six months in a young offender institution. As a result of overcrowding and staff shortages he serves the bulk of his sentence locked in a cell for 22 hours a day with two men who are doing time for armed robbery.

Upon release Nimrod is unable to secure employment and quickly drifts back into car theft. He is apprehended but when he appears in court his probation officer argues that perhaps Nimrod would respond to something completely different and recommends IT as an alternative to a custodial sentence. At this IT project he successfully completes the City and Guilds Certificate in Auto engineering.

This fairytale illustrates the reality that the system careers of most apprehended young offenders tend to escalate. The more they do the more they get. While the crimes they perpetrate may stay the same, the punishments deemed to fit them are calculated on the basis of the persistence of the offender rather than the seriousness of the offence. The probation officer in this story attempts to move Nimrod back 'down tariff'. Workers may attempt to do this when, as often happens, both the court and the young offender become locked into the logic of escalation and become similarly fatalistic about the possibility of positive change.

The story also illustrates the ambiguous position of IT. Much of the controversy about IT concerns where it should be located in the tariff of the local juvenile justice system. In our example it was used as an adjunct to front-end diversion, offering an incentive to the police youth and community bureau to make greater use of the caution. It was at the same time a project which attempted to 'prevent' future offending by offering deprived young offenders 'compensatory' experiences. It appears again as a strategic alternative to a short custodial sentence, and finally as a last resort when everything, including a substantial custodial sentence, has failed.

As we have seen, the tariff varies from area to area and this variation is determined by the beliefs and attitudes of the agents of the system, the relationships between them, the availability, or otherwise, of resources and the ages and racial origins of the children and young people who appear in court. In most local juvenile justice systems we would expect to find separate sub-tariffs in operation for white boys and black boys aged between 10 and 14; white boys and black boys aged between 14 and 17; boys and girls in both age groups and white girls and black girls.

Relatively few girls enter the juvenile justice system. (In 1986, 2467 per 100 000 girls aged between 10 and 17 were found guilty or charged for indictable offences, as against 11 571 boys.) The system they enter is different in a number of ways. For one thing it contains fewer options. There is, for example, only one girls' attendance centre in all of England and Wales, in Romford in Essex. Much IT provision is geared to the needs of boys and many young women are understandably reluctant to be the only girl at a project. Until 1988, when they were at last abandoned by the Home Office, there were no Detention Centres for girls. This has meant that the tariff for girls has a yawning gap between the discharge, fine, and supervision order at one end and the much more serious Care Order or committal to a young offender institution at the other. The few girls who do offend persistently may suddenly find themselves 'leapfrogging' from one end of the tariff to the other. This places them at a serious disadvantage in relation to their male counterparts.

The other disadvantage they face is that a much higher proportion of persistent female young offenders are deemed to be 'in moral danger' than young males. While it might be true that, in general, young women are more vulnerable to sexual exploitation by unscrupulous adults, these anxieties about the moral conduct of particular young women render them much more vulnerable to confinement in a child-care or custodial institution irrespective of the severity of their offence (Smart, 1976). The double standard towards male and female sexuality in the social world at large disadvantages young women when they enter the juvenile criminal justice system.

The juvenile justice system is a mechanism composed of a multiplicity of agents and agencies which strives to prevent, compensate, educate, divert, deter, frighten and punish children and young people in an attempt to stop them offending. When it grows weary of this endeavour it expels them to the institutions which symbolise the limits of social tolerance in this society. It is the contention of this book that we live in a remarkably intolerant society and in consequence the target of many of our interventions must be the juvenile criminal justice system itself.

5

Making an Assessment and Planning an Intervention

The nature of assessment

A social work assessment is an analysis of the ways in which the various elements of a problematic social situation interconnect. This analysis enables us to identify the most appropriate targets for, and levels of, intervention. It also enables us to specify the roles which we, and others, will play, and the most appropriate time-scales in which the various parts of our intervention can be undertaken.

Traditionally, social workers trying to understand the dynamics of a child's offending have tended to confine themselves to assessments of individual offenders and their families. As we have learnt more about the impact of the social, administrative and political systems in which our clients live, and of which both they and we are a part, the harder it has become to justify a practice which fails to address these other determinants of their social predicament. As we have observed, a critical analysis of the juvenile justice system suggests that an effective response to a child or young person in trouble may involve intervention at political and administrative, as well as face-to-face, levels.

In Chapters 2 and 3 we saw that these changing approaches to the analysis of problems is not just a consequence of the changing nature of the problems. They are a product of the development of new theories or the revival of old ones. Assessment is not a process in which we simply stand to one side of a problematic situation and objectively note its characteristics and peculiarities. What gets taken into account, and what does not, may be determined as much by the attitudes held by the worker as by the characteristics of the child or young person being assessed.

Ideally, the assessment should be a forum in which hypotheses are devised and theories tested; a place where conflicting ideas are encouraged. The totally 'objective' assessment remains an elusive ideal. We cannot offer such absolute objectivity but we can observe 'scientific' protocols in which we embark on the task of assessment with scepticism and a preparedness to test and, if necessary, discard our best ideas and firmly held convictions. During the process of assessment a supportive team of colleagues and rigorous supervision will be invaluable in enabling us to bring together our experience and our feelings.

The minimalist critique maintains that it is an over-reliance on information from the internal world of the feelings which makes social work a dubious endeavour. They suggest that, instead, social workers should adopt rigorous, scientifically authenticated, techniques of behavioural modification the results of which can be quantified (Brewer and Lait, 1980).

These criticisms betray a misunderstanding of the nature of social work, the meaning of subjectivity and the significance of feelings and this is because they are based upon a misunderstanding of the ways in which we come to acquire social knowledge. In their insistence on the superiority of models of assessment and intervention which ape the protocols of the natural sciences they obscure the important differences between the natural and the social sciences. Whereas the job of the natural sciences is, by and large, to discover cause and effect relationships in the natural world, the job of the social sciences is to ascribe *meaning* to social events. Often only by feeling what it is like to be a part of, or close to, a bewildering social situation and then stepping back and trying to conceptualise those feelings, can we achieve a level of understanding of the situation which does justice to its complexity (see for example Whyte, 1955; and Pearson, 1988).

Subjective knowledge, is indispensible in helping us to develop hypotheses about problematic social situations. We then proceed to test these hypotheses tentatively and sensitively with our clients. The subjectivity of our knowledge is not a problem, indeed this is what makes it valuable. It only becomes problematic if we fail to treat it with the same intellectual rigour with which we treat 'objective' material from the external world of events. The problem for those who insist upon what they, somewhat paradoxically, call 'total objectivity' is that they end up with only half of the picture.

The three problems confronting us at the point of assessment can be stated thus:

First, how can we build an appreciation of the social, political and administrative forces which contribute to the problem into a coherent assessment?

Second, how can we link this appreciation with our perception of the ways in which the child or young person experiences their world and themselves in it?

Third, how can we devise an intervention which addresses all these dimensions of the problem without ourselves becoming overwhelmed by the enormity and impracticality of the task?

The framework of assessment

We have to place our observations in a framework which offers clarity without obscuring or denying the complexity of our client's predicament. We must so arrange our material that we can identify those components of the problematic situation which constitute the 'network' which sustains the problem and those components, possibly the same ones, which can be mobilised to ameliorate, or indeed solve it. Robin Skynner (1971) says that we can establish what should comprise this network by asking, who is disturbed; who is disturbing; who has the motivation to alter the situation; and who has the capacity to alter the situation? 'Four different people may be involved here, or one. If the former, we are in for trouble and disappointment if we follow our usual individual-centred procedure. Within each network we must locate the main need or motivation, or we will waste our time on concentrating on the wrong part of the network or ignoring some crucial aspect of it' (p. 6).

He argues that our task in assessment is to identify the 'minimum sufficient network' which sustains any given problem, and must be dealt with if the problem is to be solved. He writes:

> The word network as I shall use it here, refers to a set of psychological structures which need to be connected to one another if the total system is to be autonomous-that is capable of intelligent response and adaptation. . . .
>
> The addition of the words 'Minimum Sufficient' indicates that we must include as much of the network as is essential to achieve our aim, but that we do not wish to make our task more complex than is absolutely necessary and so wish to exclude from consideration any elements whose influence is sufficiently small to permit them to be safely ignored (p. 3).

The minimum sufficient solution to Philip's truancy

Philip had not been attending school. Eventually this came to the attention of the EWS. Kathy, an educational welfare officer, visited Philip's family. His parents said that Philip was 'a well-behaved, obedient and happy boy at home' and they were at a loss to explain his truancy. Kathy, the worker, felt that Philip was somewhat withdrawn and appeared frightened of going to school. She visited the school and spoke to his form teacher and the year head. They said that they found Philip, when they could find him at all, 'anxious, and sometimes very distracted'.

In an interview, Philip spoke about the dreadful punishments his teachers inflicted upon pupils. He said that these things had never happened to him, and he couldn't name anybody to whom they had, but he knew they happened.

The worker was getting three, very different, accounts of events. She decided, in the manner of Skynner, that this 'set of psychological structures needed to be connected with each other if the total system (was) to be . . . capable of intelligent response and adaptation'. She arranged a meeting between Philip, his mother and father, Philip's form teacher and the year head.

In the meeting is emerged that Philip had learned of the awful punishments inflicted at school from his mother and father. His anxieties were reinforced when teachers, annoyed by Philip's sporadic attendances and poor concentration, would utter vague, but nonetheless alarming, threats about what would happen to him if he continued to truant.

As a result of this meeting Kathy devised a two-part intervention.

The first part was dealt with in a meeting between Philip, his year head and herself to devise a contract about Philip's attendance which specified his rights and obligations, and those of the teachers as well. It specified sanctions which would be invoked for non-attendance which proved to be a great deal less alarming than Philip's fantasies.

The second part involved sessions with Philip and his parents. Here, Kathy tried to help them locate the sources of their own fears of school. She tried to help the parents understand the consequences for Philip of projecting their own fears about authority onto the school. She then encouraged them to think about how they would come to terms with their own authority and use it to make Philip feel secure at school and at home.

The content of assessment

Charles Critchter (1975) argues that we can only begin to understand an individual's involvement in crime if we address their behaviour at the levels of Structure, Culture and Biography simultaneously. He writes:

> For us, biography is the network of personal circumstances, decisions, and (mis)fortunes which occur within a situation already highly structured and with a limited number of available cultural options (p. 170).
>
> It may ultimately be that biographical factors (including some conscious choice) are crucial in the final thrust towards criminal activity, but the problems which the crime 'acts out' have been set by the interaction of structural and cultural factors over and above the individual actor (p. 171).

This alerts us to the importance of not individualising social problems.

Ken Pryce (1979) has argued that colonialism and economics have conspired to locate black young people in Britain at a point in the social structure where they are subjected to 'Endless Pressure'. Bombarded with exhortations from the media, the educational system and the government to achieve, they are denied the legitimate occupational and educational opportunities which would enable them to do so.

This ever-present tendency became accentuated during the long economic recession of the 1970s and 1980s. In almost all western societies this structural double-bind triggered an upsurge of crimes of poverty amongst young people who experienced relative deprivation most accutely (Cloward and Ohlin, 1960; Lee and Young, 1984). This phenomenon is now a structural feature of most advanced industrial societies. Paul Webster (1988) writes: 'Racial tension, underlined by the fact that Mr Jean-Marie Le Penn scored 20% in Les Minguettes in the presidential election this year, was at the base of the rioting and the high delinquency rate in which 7,200 cases were reported in the peak year of 1983. Like delinquency, every statistic can almost automatically be translated into racial terms' (*Guardian*, 5 September 1988, p. 19).

These remarkable social phenomena are all-too-readily incorporated into our taken-for-granted assumptions about the way the world is. Yet an understanding that an individual's structural position limits his or her options and predisposes such a person to an involvement in crime should not obscure the reality that this involvement is not inevitable.

The assumption of inevitability means that we fail to ask the most important (structural) questions like, why boys? why not girls? why the poor? why here? and why now? Yet if we fail to ask these questions in our assessments we preclude, from the outset, the possibility of being able to devise a realistic response to the social, as opposed to individual, reality of juvenile offending.

We can ask these questions and construct realistic responses if the information gained for our assessments feeds into a broader process of monitoring and assessing offences, disposals, resources and opportunities in the area. These processes are normally developed as a result of policies and strategies formulated at agency and inter-agency level in the district, borough or county in which we work (Thorpe, 1980; NACRO, 1988).

A useful exercise which can be undertaken, at minimal cost, in an area office and which will complement, and give direction to, systems monitoring initiatives and the work of inter-agency panels involves sticking coloured pins into a map of the district. This will indicate where the offenders come from, where their offences are committed and, if we suspect that there may be a problem in the school, where they receive their education (Power, 1972). This information can be elaborated by plotting on a graph the times in the day, the days in the week and the weeks in the year, when all, or particular types of, offences occur. This very simple form of information gathering can give us some indication of who does what, to whom, when and where, and it will, almost certainly, reveal patterns. These patterns will reveal where the victims and the perpetrators are clustered. They will give us a clue to the informal adolescent networks of which local children and young people in trouble are a part and the estates, streets, cafés and pubs in which they meet. This level of assessment offers us the type of information we need to launch an intervention which, while not individualising the problems of juvenile crime and victimisation, responds to the needs and problems of individuals caught up in it.

Three examples of the efficacy of sticking pins in a map

1. Having located the estates on which most of the young people passing through the local juvenile justice system lived by sticking pins in a map, social workers in an area office in south-east London persuaded their department to designate a social worker to work half-time as a detached worker with young people in these areas. He worked in conjunction with a youth worker from a local settlement house. Together they made contact with networks of young people and developed a range of formal and informal counselling, group-work and advisory services. These services were used for prevention and diversion, and as an alternative to custody. This resulted in an appreciable reduction in crime, and in the numbers of youngsters entering the juvenile justice system, and care and custody. This echoes the experience of the étés jeunes *in France and the Safe Neighbourhoods projects in Britain, namely that services developed with young people, on a highly localised basis, work.*

2. The manager of a branch of a large chain store in a small northern town was informed by researchers investigating local patterns of juvenile crime that according to a self-report study his store was the one most prone to pilfering and that this reached its peak between 4 pm and 5.30 pm on weekdays. The store manager discussed this problem with the researchers and a local voluntary agency working with young offenders. As a result an after-school club was established which kept the children busy until the store shut. The club was funded by the store but it cost only about 25 per cent of the amount which was saved as a result of the reduction in the level of pilfering. The level of prosecutions for shoplifting also dropped appreciably.

3. An inter-agency consultative group in south-west London monitored local patterns of juvenile offending and noted that bag snatching was concentrated in a crowded street market on Saturday mornings. Police stuck posters on walls in the area, alerted stall-holders and customers to the dangers by approaching people who were making themselves particularly vulnerable to these offences and they assumed a more obvious presence on Saturdays. They also let it be known on the estates and in the schools where most of the known perpetrators came from that they were doing this. The incidence of bag snatching dropped markedly, as did prosecutions.

These are examples of responses to structural pressures towards offending. It is evident, however, that while social structure determines who gets dealt which cards, it is the interplay between culture and biography which determines how they are played.

Culture

The concept of culture is challenging 'community' as the social work word which means least but has fewest negative connotations. Far too often 'culture' is invoked not as an explanation but as an indication that no further explanation is necessary. A person's culture is a central prop to their identity and as such a consideration of culture is a key element in the social work assessment. This is why we must use the concept of 'culture' carefully.

Shama Ahmed (1986) identifies five potential pitfalls which face those who rely too heavily upon cultural explanations of social phenomena.

There is a danger that we can *over-simplify* and generalise from an unexamined stereotype. It is, for example, an accepted part of white law-and-order folklore that whereas Afro-Caribbean young people are over-represented in the criminal statistics, the more passive Asians are not, because their culture discourages such expressions of masculine aggression. As a result it took criminology and social work an inordinately long time to cotton on to the fact that as the economic circumstances of the less privileged sections of second-generation male Asian youth worsened so their involvement in crime began to increase. This phenomenon threatens to drive a coach and horses through theories which explain the differential involvement of separate racial groups in crime in terms of cultural predisposition. It has, or it should have, forced us back to a consideration of the economic predicament, and the experience of relative deprivation, of these groups.

We also have to be clear about what does, and what does not, constitute *normality* within a culture. For instance, it is regarded as neither normal nor acceptable within white working-class culture for young men to steal cars, nor is it acceptable in the Afro-Caribbean community for young men to supplement their income through street crime. Unless we are able to distinguish between the cultural and the intolerable we end up perpetuating dangerous stereotypes in the way that Cashmore and Troyna (1982) do. In an attempt to account for a marked rise in prosecutions of black young people for street crime in Birmingham in the late 1970s they argue 'that there is a penchant for violence within the West Indian culture, possibly stemming from the days of slavery' (pp. 32–3).

What they fail to tell us is how this cultural penchant has survived the years since the abolition of slavery, why it has leapt at least three generations, why most black young people don't do it, why some white young people whose ancestors were never enslaved do, and why it arrived in Birmingham in the late 1970s to afflict a small group of black British adolescents most of whom had never set foot on a Caribbean island. The problem with this account is that it ignores the contemporary structural constraints upon these young people, and the role of individual biography, as key determinants of deviant motivation. What it also ignores, of course, is the crucial role played by the police and the courts in identifying culprits and defining offences.

Such simplistic culturalist explanations can result in the *masking of real emotional difficulties* experienced by a young person.

Leila's stereotypical mugger

Leila was allocated the case of Derek, a 16-year-old boy of Afro-Caribbean origin who was facing probable imprisonment as a result of being arrested for the third time for robbing elderly white women. These offences were all committed in circumstances in which detection and identification were almost inevitable.

On her home visit Leila was struck by the fact that Derek's parents who were law-abiding church-going people said that they thought Derek was a bad boy for doing what he had done but managed to do this in a way which did not communicate disapproval. They also said that if Derek had been brought up 'at home', in the West Indies, none of this would have happened, suggesting that the problem might be a consequence of a clash of cultural values.

Leila asked Derek's parents if they had ever experienced any racism or prejudice and they said that in the 25 years that they had spent in this country they had never once experienced it. Leila said that, as a black person, she experienced quite a lot of it and gave a few examples, but Derek's parents said that nothing like that had ever happened to them.

In her subsequent office interview Leila asked Derek why he committed offences which corresponded so closely with popular racist stereotypes of what black youths were supposed to be like. She also asked him why he was apparently asking to get caught. Derek said he did it because he was bad and that he was just unlucky to get caught. Leila asked Derek how he got on with his parents. He said that he loved them, felt responsible for them and ashamed that he had upset them. Like his parents, Derek said the words without feeling. Leila said that they didn't seem very upset. Derek said they never did but he always knew that they were. Leila asked Derek what he thought would happen to him. He said, 'I will have to go away'. Leila asked Derek if he would be prepared to consider an alternative to custody project if the court could be persuaded to entertain this idea but he said, 'I have to go away'.

Leila asked Derek how he would like his parents to react. He thought hard, and then he said, with emotion, 'I'd like them to get really angry and tell me not to do it ever again'. After this Derek said that he would be interested in an alternative to custody.

Leila felt that Derek was trapped in the 'bad black boy' role which he had learnt from the popular press. She thought that his job in the family was to express the anger, frustration and hurt which his parents had felt it necessary to deny. They had kept their heads down, kept their tempers, and tried to pass as white for 25 years. Derek adopted a high profile, expressed his anger and was bad and black.

At the next meeting with Derek and his parents Leila talked with the family about the work that she felt they had to do in owning their own feelings about their bad experiences so that Derek could be free to get on with the difficult task of finding his own place in a white, racist society.

Derek's difficulties also illustrate the other two dangers, identified by Shama Ahmed: 'that a preoccupation with cultural conflict may lead to a denial of the *crisis of racial identity* and self-image' (p. 149) or a *desire to resist racism* (my italics).

Biography

The cross-over between the biographical and the cultural is in the subcultures which evolve from, and act out aspects of, the dominant culture. These subcultures account for the peculiarities of particular families, peer groups and institutions – schools, churches and children's homes – and have a powerful impact upon the kinds of people we become.

George Herbert Mead (1934) observed that we discover who we are through our interactions with, and the information we receive back from, the 'significant others' around us. To that extent our 'individual' identity is a social product. This does not mean that we have no hand in deciding the kind of person we become or that we have no responsibility for it. What it does mean, is that if we wish to make sense of individual behaviour we must address the 'system', usually the family system, which helped to make the person the way they are and may well have an investment in keeping them that way.

R. D. Laing's research into the functioning of the families of people diagnosed as schizophrenic explored the more sinister aspects of the process by which individual identity is constructed. He demonstrated that serious unresolved problems within families may be rediscovered as the personal attributes of the identified patient and projected onto them. The identified patient obligingly internalises these projections and goes mad, making the family feel a great deal better and the patient a great deal worse.

Having identified the structural and cultural factors which predispose a child or young person to seek a delinquent solution to their problem, our task is to ascertain what, in Crichter's phrase, constitutes 'the final thrust towards criminal activity'. We may find, as we did in Derek's case, that unresolved problems within the family sometimes open the way for a structurally and culturally scripted set of events to unfold. But clearly the same structure and the multiplicity of cultures which emerge within it can generate a huge variety of social scripts.

Cultural options exist and individual choice is a reality, but so is social constraint. Paul Willis (1977) draws our attention to the very different attitudes to education expressed by the lads and the 'lobes' who are, respectively, the disreputable and the respectable denizens of the working-class classroom. The lobes maintain an upwardly-mobile orientation taking on the cultural values of the school which emphasise intellectual effort and conformity. The lads, in contrast, 'dig in' at the back of the class and celebrate the virtues of hard manual labour, toughness and wit, noisily and persistently from the beginning of the third year onwards.

These different options were both solutions to the strain the boys experienced between the conflicting imperatives of the culture of the home and the working-class neighbourhood, and the culture of the school. This radical differentiation is not inevitable and where it occurs it tends to be fostered by teaching staff and the judgements they make about the abilities of their pupils.

Children and young people tend to act as they are treated. They do this because in most situations they have very limited power. If they are treated as stupid, or clumsy, clever or beautiful by significant others then they are very likely to act as if they were. While it is of course true that a person's self-image will have some basis in objective reality – some people are taller than others, some are more intelligent, some have more money – what we make of these objective differences will be shaped by our subjective feelings and beliefs about who we are and what we are worth, by our self-image.

Structure and culture, as we have seen, will delimit the opportunities available to us but biography, the process through which our self-image is constructed, will tell us if we are the kind of person who can take advantage of the limited opportunities available. If, like many working-class and black young people, our biographical experience has led us to see ourselves as academic failures, then the opportunity to improve our employment prospects by studying for exams at evening classes will, for us, be just another chance to fail.

Social work assessment with young offenders is often concerned with discovering how their biographies have been spoiled and how we might create experiences which will offer the child or young person an alternative, compensatory, source of positive feedback.

The framework of intervention

As we have seen, because we are almost invariably working with people whose chances and choices are highly structured by social inequality our assessment is likely to indicate interventions at political and administrative, as well as face-to-face, levels. If, as Crichter suggests, individual incidents of juvenile crime are most usefully regarded as behaviour which acts out pre-given social problems then one of our jobs will be to help transform the ensemble of these 'private troubles' into 'public issues' (Hall, S. and Jefferson, T., 1976).

Pincus and Minnahan (1973) offer useful terms with which to identify the different components of the minimum sufficient network when they distinguish between client systems, change-agent systems, target systems, and action systems.

The clients and the change agents

At a common sense level social work is an activity in which a social worker acts as the 'agent' of the 'client' in furtherance of a set of mutually agreed goals. This agent has a contract, maintains confidentiality with, acts at the behest and in the interests of, and owes first and unfailing loyalty to, the client.

We have already noted that real life in the juvenile justice system is more complicated than this and the above account tells us more about the limitations of common sense than it does about the role of the social worker. Social workers execute statutory orders as an agent of the court. As public professionals they must work in what they assume to be the best interests of an elusive, anonymous, but important client called 'the community'. It is this client, of course, which is the target of the crime perpetrated by the other client, the young offender.

Beyond this are further complications which become evident in the all-too-familiar situation in which a young offender, his parents, and the magistrate each has a different preferred outcome in a case and a legitimate claim to have these preferences taken into account by the social worker.

In this stressful and potentially confusing situation the intervention may of necessity be a compromise. The compromise intervention will be shaped by the negotiation the social worker conducts between the competing claims of the interested parties in an attempt to set up an intervention which addresses the problems identified in the assessment. It is crucial that our assessment considers the range of 'clients' to whom we will be accountable in our intervention, what this means in terms of the information we will share with them and the confidentiality we can offer them. This in turn raises the question of how this, often highly complicated, matrix of potentially conflicting accountabilities will be presented to each of our 'clients'.

Targets

The target for intervention will be determined by where we believe the problem and the solution reside. 'Reside' is the key term because while it may be the case that a young person's problem has its origins in the damage wrought by a negligent upbringing and that the family might in some way be identified as the ultimate cause of the problem it does not follow that the problem, or its solution, resides within the family.

Family therapy which was pioneered as a mode of intervention with the families of persistent offenders, has become very popular with social workers in the recent period. Therapists have found that the families of persistent juvenile offenders are characterised by a great deal of ambiguity about roles and 'boundaries' and this offers us an interesting insight into some of the factors which have helped to sustain their deviant careers. Family therapy has not been demonstrably successful in checking these careers, however. This is not because its analysis of the factors which may have precipitated, and served to maintain, particular kinds of behaviour is necessarily wrong but because the solution, if one exists, does not reside within the family.

In our attempts to identify the target for our intervention we should avoid being misled by what we assume to be normality. We cannot assume that the system which we 'normally' expect to be most significant for a child or young person will, in fact, be so.

There are enough examples of situations in which the best friend, the lover or the peer group of a young offender contain their criminal behaviour, meet their emotional needs and offer them an alternative mode of expression, to make us wary of reifying the family in this way (Pearson, 1974). Increasingly social workers in the fields of eating disorders, drug addiction and persistent offending, are abandoning the family as a target for intervention and focusing instead upon helping young people to separate from their families and transfer their dependency to people and groups more able to respond to their needs.

As we have noted, private troubles, manifested in the family, may also be instances of public issues which have an administrative or political remedy. As a result we may often find it necessary simultaneously to target our interventions at political, administrative and face-to-face levels. In doing this we will often be working indirectly through activists who operate at a variety of different levels in a range of agencies and systems.

The Action System

The Action System is composed of the individuals, groups and agencies (the activists) we are able to mobilise to further the goals of our intervention. They may be the young offenders themselves, their teachers, the staff of an IT centre, the Director of Social Services who institutes meetings with the local police or the bench, or the young offender's peer group. Whoever they are, what they have in common is that they are the people who take the action which we have identified as necessary in our assessment. Through their actions at political, administrative and face-to-face levels they try to stop a bad situaiton getting worse, or to change that situation for the better. The change agent may be an activist herself, but very often she will be working behind the scenes to support the activists who are making the intervention. This support is very important because if social workers expect activists to act for them they, in turn, have a right to expect clear communication, and support. If an adventure-playground worker has spent a gruelling day containing the idiosyncratic behaviour of one of a demanding juvenile client, he or she deserves half an hour of the social worker's time in which to talk about his or her difficulties, and probably a pint as well if the department can run to it.

The time-scale of intervention

Interventions at different levels will usually operate according to different time-scales.

A social worker writes a social enquiry report about a black youngster charged with threatening behaviour, and successfully recommends an absolute discharge. This involves working on the case for a total of two days. It takes over a year of lobbying and behind-the-scenes work before the issue of the apparent reluctance of the police to caution black young people can be placed on the agende of an inter-agency juvenile liaison group. Members of the local IT association, in conjunction with the NALGO social work section, are writing a contribution to a report on the policing of ethnic minority young people, which is being orchestrated by a national youth pressure group, for the European Commission. It could take four years before anything appears in print.

The overall objective of these interventions is to promote justice for, and the welfare of, youngsters in trouble. It is conducted at different levels and on different time-scales but the effectiveness of each of its parts is dependant on the effectiveness of them all.

The content of intervention

The next four chapters deal with the content of interventions. In Chapters 7, 8 and 9 work undertaken directly by the change agent, or by other activists, to achieve the goals of the intervention is addressed. Chapter 10 considers how change can be effected through intervention at administrative and political levels.

The danger of fashionable solutions (a cautionary note)

Perhaps because social workers usually operate on the borderline between the known and the unknown and are therefore prone to the anxiety which such 'dangerous' living engenders, they are prey to fashionable theories and methods of intervention which offer to inject a greater degree of certainty into their endeavours.

In recent times we have been presented with a succession of novel interventions which were 'sold' on the basis that they addressed problems which earlier, less sophisticated, methods had failed to reach. These panaceas normally had about four good years and a couple of lean ones before they reluctantly relinquished their claims to universal applicability and accepted that while they might be appropriate for some clients there were quite a few who were 'unable to use this type of help'. In recent times we have seen the emergence of *brief focal work*, *social skills training*, *behavioural contracts*, the *correctional* (recently re-designated the '*offending*') *curriculum* and *family therapy* as contenders for the title of the 'best, and probably the only sensible, social work intervention with young offenders'.

Fashionable theories in their early days are solutions in search of problems to which they can be an answer. The dangers in this are two-fold. Firstly it may result in a client being subjected to an unsuitable intervention because of the worker's desire to 'have a go' at the novel method. Second, clients who are regarded as unsuitable candidates for new and popular methods tend to get dealt with by old unpopular ones. All too often, the new panaceas have revealed, on closer inspection, a propensity inadvertently to harm the 'untreatable' residue who weren't clever enough, good enough or bad enough to serve as the raw material of the method. As Richard Titmuss has observed, 'the denial of complexity' can be 'the essence of tyranny' and sometimes it has been youngsters in trouble who have paid the price for the reluctance of some of the proponents of new methods to acknowledge their limitations. More than one young person has been imprisoned because social workers felt they would not respond to the particular form of treatment favoured by the agency.

We don't know enough about methods of intervention, and we certainly don't know enough about children and young people in trouble, to prescribe methods of intervention as if they were a course of tablets. Doing social work with young offenders involves responding to them in their uniqueness and their diversity. It means starting with them where they are and exploring, and sometimes inventing, ways of working with them. If social workers reverse this process and try to slot young offenders into their favourite method of intervention, irrespective of the young person's needs and wishes, while they might be helping their own careers along they may be doing young people a great deal of harm.

6

Working with the Court

The social work role in court

Social workers often make their first contact with a young offender when their (delinquent) 'solution' has turned into a problem and the social worker has to write a report about it.

Social workers receive requests for social enquiry reports (SERs) from the juvenile bench, either because magistrates feel that the social circumstances or personal difficulties of a young person indicate that he or she may be in need of specialised help, or because they are thinking of imposing a custodial sentence and are therefore required by law to institute such inquiries. Magistrates expect social workers, on the basis of their knowledge of the social sciences and social work method, to give 'value-free', 'expert' opinions and recommendations about the impact of any sentence the court may wish to impose. There is moreover, often an assumption on the part of the bench that in arriving at their recommendations social workers will have had an eye to the competing claims of 'justice', which must be seen to be done, compensation or vindication of the victims, deterrence of other potential offenders, punishment of the wrong-doer, and the needs and best interests of the young offender.

While social workers do usually take these factors into account, the idea that they are disinterested experts is something of a myth. This is because it is based upon the erroneous assumption that a system built upon a foundation of profound ideological and theoretical conflict can generate neutral, or value-free, outcomes. It ignores the tension for social workers between their role as servants of the court and their other role as people who are professionally bound to work in the best interests of the client. When juvenile court magistrates, acting in what they believe to be the best interest of the community, imprison a young offender, they are almost invariably not advancing the young person's best interest as defined by social workers.

These differences in orientation between magistrates and social workers, and the conflict it engenders, have been a major cause of the decline in the use of the supervision order, and the neglect of the Intermediate Treatment requirement as a juvenile court disposal, in the past decade or so. Magistrates as a body have consistently demanded that a social worker who is supervising young offenders should exert some surveillance and control over their behaviour. Social workers are, however, members of a profession built upon the core values of 'client self-determination', 'confidentiality' and 'respect for persons', irrespective of the choices they make or the actions they take. Sometimes, as is the case in the juvenile justice system, there is considerable tension between these professional values and the setting in which the profession is practised. There may also be a tension between the theoretical explanations of offending offered to social workers by the social sciences and the beliefs held by magistrates.

The problem of responsibility

One of the reasons a magistrate will ask a social worker to provide an assessment of the personality, character and family and social background of a young offender is to establish the extent to which they were responsible for their actions.

Matza (1964) suggests that this task is problematic in practice because young offenders seldom, if ever, resemble either the free legal subject so dear to the hearts of lawyers or the determined social object beloved of behavioural psychologists. He argues that delinquents are neither wholly free not wholly determined. Rather their capacity to exert a free and rational choice is impaired.

This helps to explain why many of the young people we meet professionally seem perplexed about how they ended up in so much trouble. It would be naive to ignore the fact that this apparent confusion can be a very convenient rationalisation, but listening to their accounts of what happened we are often left with the feeling that in some way the offence 'happened to' the young person. There is seldom a sense of a calculating actor embarking upon a freely-chosen course of action.

Most juvenile crime is, in reality, an ill-conceived shambles. Young people may well be responsible for an offence but it is hard to extrapolate from their accounts the precise moment at which a choice was made or a decision taken. In their stories things just happen. Once events are set in train any possibility of exerting control over them seems to evaporate.

Persistent offenders are more often than not people who have little experience of making things happen. They have been denied the means to become the authors of their own lives. Their socia' position, having granted them responsibility for nothing renders them effectively irresponsible. Social workers by trying to affect their social circumstances, and by confronting young offenders with the issue of choice, attempt to restore to them the responsibility which the limitations of their past experiences may have denied them. Social work with young offenders often involves persuading the court to confront a more complex social reality than those suggested by the twin fictions of the legalistic and 'scientific' world-views, and to accept the validity of their attempts to expand the range of solutions available to young offenders.

This latter process can begin in the first encounter between the young person and the worker when the worker is preparing the SER. In doing this, however, it is important for the worker to acknowledge that the authority he or she carries as an officer of the court will affect the type of relationship he or she will be able to develop with a child or young person in trouble.

Authority

Because most young offenders are able to draw upon a rich legacy of sub-cultural defences in their dealings with people in authority they often have much less of a problem with it than their social workers. The problem for social workers is not, as is sometimes suggested, that their authority creates a barrier to the development of a good relationship with the young offender. That barrier, if it didn't exist already, went up as soon as the young person was apprehended. It is the barrier which inevitably separates those who break the law from those who are paid to uphold it.

The task of the social worker is to respond honestly to these defences which, like all defences, are adaptations to a problematic reality. What both the client and the worker know is that they would probably never have met if one of them hadn't broken the law and this acknowledgement is a realistic starting point for the first interview. What is less clear to young people in this predicament, who are often suspicious and frightened, is why they have to talk to a social worker and what the worker can do to, and for, them.

Central to this task is the clarification of the choices available to, and the respective responsibilities of, the social worker and the young offender. Social workers don't stop young people offending. If they do stop, they stop themselves. By engaging the young offender as an active and responsible participant in the production of the SER, rather than just the passive subject of it, we can help them to develop the capacity to do this. As part of this process it can be useful at the SER stage to agree a simple interim contract with the child or young person in trouble which covers their own and the worker's rights and responsibilities in the period prior to their court appearance.

The contract below was agreed between Beverly, the social worker and Brian, a 15-year-old on a burglary charge.

Beverly agrees:

1. To help Brian to find a solicitor to represent him in court.
2. That, having gathered the information I need for the production of my SER, I will discuss my impressions with Brian and give him a chance to correct any mistakes and to discuss in full anything that he doesn't agree with.
3. To then discuss the recommendation/s I am considering and, if possible, to negotiate it with Brian.
4. To give Brian an honest opinion about the most likely outcome/s of his forthcoming court appearance and what will be expected of him, including the penalties for non-compliance, if my recommendation is accepted.
5. To give Brian ample opportunity to read my SER prior to his court appearance, to explain anything he doesn't understand about it and to give him one copy for himself and one for his solicitor.

Brian agrees:

1. To keep appointments with Beverly and any other appointments (IT for example) which she arranges for me.
2. To decide whether or not to participate in any IT scheme, or other alternative to custody, which I may be offered.
3. To think about what is on offer and to come to a meeting with Beverly with suggestions about the programme which will best meet my needs, or at least that I am prepared to participate in.
4. To discuss Beverly's recommendation and to tell her the measures I am prepared to comply with.
5. To appear in court.

The young offenders family

Magistrates usually want an account of a child or young person's home circumstances and family relationships in order to establish whether the family is willing or able to help keep the young person out of trouble. The worker discusses with the family what they would be willing to do if the court were to require it of them. It is important that, whatever this is, the family has both the capacity and the motivation to do it. The worker who encourages families to agree to unrealistic plans may be setting-up the family, and the young person, for future failure, a failure moreover, which could lead to their eventual incarceration. If the family is to engage in some work it must be work on something that they see as problematic. An appreciation of the psychodynamics of school refusal may consistently elude families who may nonetheless fall into a discussion of whose job it is to set the alarm clock with a will. To work effectively with young offenders and their families, or with any other group of people, we need to match our intervention to their concerns and to present it in a way that they can understand and use.

There will be occasions when the family will not support the young offender. By its indifference about what happens to him or its collusion with his offending, it will push him towards a deeper involvement in crime and the harsher penalties which are a consequence of this involvement. In these circumstances the role of the worker prior to the court appearance is to offer the support the family is unwilling or unable to give. In considering a recommendation the worker can try to engage the young person in a discussion of alternative sources of support and emotional satisfaction. Too often children and young people in the juvenile court are placed in CHEs because their parents are not interested in them. The job of the worker preparing the SER is not simply to deliver the dismal news about the family but to investigate with the young person alternative sources of support which can be mobilised to compensate for it; to find, in short, a new solution.

Magistrates may ask the social services department to supply them with full reports. In which case the child's school, an assessment centre, an educational psychologist, a psychiatrist, and the social services department IT section, may all be asked for their view of the young offender. The role of social workers differs from that of other professionals who supply information to the court in that they are not simply expert witnesses but sentencing advisers to the bench as well. Other professionals are asked to give a view of the character, and attitudes of a defendant. Social workers, on the basis of their own inquiries and the information supplied by these other professionals, are required to recommend what should happen to a young offender. Social workers play a crucial role in these deliberations. Research shows more than a 75 per cent correspondence between what social workers recommend and what magistrates decide to do. How social workers conceive of their role in the court and their relationship with the bench will determine how they approach the production of their SER and the coordination and presentation of the expert opinions which are proffered.

Expert opinions

The school

Most magistrates think that a child's behaviour and attendance at school is very important and tend, as a result, to take reports from schools very seriously. These reports vary enormously in content and quality. They can be an affirmation of faith in the child's capacity for growth and change, a clinical analysis of their intellectual and motor abilities, or a 'character assassination'. Too often, unsubstantiated assertions that the child is a 'trouble-maker' or 'easily led' are presented to the courts as if they were facts. Stigmatising reports from schools can have serious consequences and may make the difference between a custodial and non-custodial sentence. Prejudicial reports from schools have been shown to accelerate the progress of black children through the juvenile justice system (NACRO, 1984).

Magistrates, like most other people, believe that teachers, by dint of the 15 000 hours or so that a child will spend in school, will know the child better than other adults (Rutter, 1978). The magistrate is therefore prone to accept school reports, even when on a closer reading the 'evidence' may appear somewhat dubious. The reality of day-to-day life in an urban comprehensive school belies the assumed intimacy of the teacher-pupil relationship. Responsibility for pastoral care is delegated to year heads. Responsibility for the control of truancy is assumed by the educational welfare service. Behavioural problems are the domain of the school counsellor, the educational psychologist, the child guidance clinic or the behavioural unit. This division of labour, compounded by staff shortages and the sheer size of the school, can mean that children in trouble may be seen by all and known by none. For the children who hover on the margins of the school it can be a cool and impersonal place. They slip easily through this elaborate network of helping resources which seems to offer everything except the warm and spontaneous relationships which, Rutter informs us, make all the difference. Sometimes it will fall to the social worker to point out to magistrates that some schools can be highly problematic places for deprived or vulnerable children and young people.

The assessment centre

Formally, juveniles should only be remanded for a residential assessment if they have committed a very serious offence, if they pose a threat to themselves or another person, or if they are likely to break bail. Unfortunately magistrates and social workers do not always use residential facilities in this way. Magistrates will sometimes remand a child or young person to a residential facility even though their offence is minor and there is no pressing need for the detailed information which professionals engaged in the assessment process produce. This apparently irrational practice usually occurs when magistrates believe they are encountering an instance of the 'affront to authority'. The 'affront to authority' is a crucial determinant of destiny in the juvenile justice system. Research shows that policemen, magistrates, teachers, social workers and prison officers throw professional judgement and caution to the four winds if they believe that the juvenile with whom they are dealing is 'taking the piss' (Cicourel, 1968; and Landau, 1981).

This temporary incarceration, intended as a salutary lesson in the value of deference to authority, can have some very serious unintended consequences however. Reinach *et al.* (1974) observed that workers in the assessment centre they studied believed that if a magistrate or a social worker had taken the serious step of removing a child from home to a residential assessment centre they must be thinking about placing them in a residential establishment in the longer term. This very reasonable assumption led them to define their task as assessing the child for a placement in a community home which would meet their needs rather than assessing whether or not the child should in fact be removed from home. This initial misapprehension was compounded by a phenomenon peculiar to residential establishments. Children and young people entering them often manifest behaviour which they have not previously, and will never subsequently, display. This behaviour, withdrawal, aggression or violence, is an uncharacteristic response to a threatening and unfamiliar situation. When such behaviour is placed in the context of a staff group searching for evidence to substantiate a recommendation of residential care, it very easily becomes a self-fulfilling prophecy.

It was the recognition of these processes, and the enormous cost of residential assessment, which led local authority social services departments in the mid-1970s to pioneer day-assessment facilities under the auspices of IT. While day assessment can minimise behavioural distortions it cannot eradicate them. Its major advantage over a residential assessment is that whereas a residential assessment can only tell us how a child or young person behaves in a residential establishment, day assessment can indicate how he or she might survive outside, in the place where he or she will eventually have to live.

The educational psychologist

The close correlation between difficulties at school and persistent involvement in juvenile crime suggests that if we are able to identify and deal with problems a child is experiencing at school this may give us some purchase on the problem of offending. The diagnosis of those problems is the job of the educational psychologist.

Educational psychologists apply tests which provide a comparison of pupils' academic and intellectual capacities and their actual attainment. These tests tell us whether children are 'underfunctioning' and, if they are, what the reasons might be. They make it possible to differentiate between the problems of two equally unhappy children, one of whom is unable to learn because of a cognitive impairment and the other who is unable to learn because of anxieties about his or her family, or the school. On the basis of these tests the educational psychologist is able to suggest the kind of remedial educational programme, counselling, or indeed school, which in their judgement, would constitute the most appropriate response to the problems they have identified. Whether the recommended option is in fact available, is another, political, question.

In recent times educational psychologists, influenced by the pioneering research undertaken in the social psychology of education in the late 1960s and 1970s by people like David Hargreaves (1967) and Michael Rutter *et al.* (1978), have tended to focus upon the dynamics of schools and classrooms as well as the difficulties of individual pupils. This change in the level of analysis, while sometimes threatening to staff, can offer teachers and social workers who are trying to locate the source of a child's difficulties at school invaluable information.

Social workers can use this information to advantage if they, or their agency, have established a dialogue with the school about the ways in which they will work together with children and young people under stress or in trouble. The relationship between social workers and the school is dealt with in Chapter 8.

On the other hand, the identification of learning difficulties, with all their connotations of 'subnormality', in a situation of sparse remedial resources can mean that a child who is also 'getting into trouble' is in danger of being despatched to a behavioural unit or a residential school for 'maladjusted' or less able children. In this way youngsters can be inducted into a 'career' in the special education system which is every bit as stigmatising as the system which deals with 'young offenders'.

The psychiatrist

Occasionally social workers encounter young offenders whose behaviour is so bizarre or at odds with reality that the usual ways of understanding their problems and responding to their needs are of no use. In these circumstances social workers or magistrates may decide to request a psychiatric assessment.

There was a period in the recent history of forensic psychiatry when almost all delinquency was seen as a symptom of mental enfeeblement or mental illness. Latterly psychiatry has begun, sometimes somewhat grudgingly, to 'normalise' the criminal, recognising that while a burglar may be a neurotic psychotic or perfectly sane, so might a cabinet minister. But the question of whether, when and in which ways a person's criminality may be a symptom of their mental condition remains. Progressive social-scientific theory has attacked and demolished many of psychiatry's taken-for-granted categories of madness. Yet, although 'psychopaths' have ceased to exist theoretically, we still face a problem when we meet somebody who behaves like psychopaths did before they became extinct (Taylor *et al.*, 1973). In these circumstances a psychiatrist may tell us no more than what we will be unable to do. This is valuable information because it makes our job safer, spares the young person further 'failures' in placements which cannot contain him, and pushes us to consider what we believe to be the best of the remaining, often somewhat bleak, options.

When social workers recommend, or magistrates request, psychiatric reports as part of an assessment, they usually do so because they are at a loss to know what to do next and hope that a psychiatrist may be able to tell them. Ironically psychiatrists, who may well be able to tell them something of the inner lives of the young people referred to them, are usually unable to throw much light upon the two questions social workers and magistrates most want answered: 'what makes them do it?' and 'what should we do with them?' However sophisticated the assessment, the answers to these questions will be provided ultimately by the magistrate who decides, often on the basis of the social worker's recommendation, what to do with a young offender, and the social worker who is sometimes responsible for carrying out their decision. Psychiatric assessment offers no respite from this responsibility, no access to additional facilities or resources and no easy answers.

Intermediate treatment (IT)

Most local authority social services departments have an IT section and in some of them the IT organiser doubles as Court Officer and is responsible for relations between the department, the police, the probation service, voluntary organisations and the juvenile court. Some IT sections offer a consultancy service to field social workers producing SERs. Whereas field workers may only ever be working with one or two young offenders the IT section does nothing else and as a result can often offer expertise and access to resources which can enable field workers to do their job more effectively. Since the implementation of the 1982 CJA, and the 'New Initiative' in IT in 1983, IT sections have been increasingly involved in the provision of reports to courts on a young person's ability or willingness to participate in, and the availability of, IT programmes. These reports, which usually follow a period of day-assessment, are essential if a court is considering a custodial sentence because, in law, ability, willingness and availability constitute reasons why a court should refrain from imposing a custodial sentence. In this situation IT fulfils the function of an alternative to custody but, as we have seen, the question of where, precisely, IT should be located on the tariff of penalties available to the court remains a vexed question.

The social worker will usually use these expert opinions as the evidence and rationale for their recommendations to the court. They may, of course, disagree with the 'experts' and if, after further discussion, they are still at odds with them, they will have to bring the disagreement to the attention of the court and explain its basis. Their role as co-ordinator of the reports gives social workers an opportunity to meet the other professionals engaged in the assessment and to offer them a broader context in which to place their observations about particular aspects of a child's life. While the 'experts' offer a view of a moment in a child or young person's life the social worker locates that moment within the overall cycle. The social worker also locates the young offender in time by linking observations about their present functioning with an understanding of their past history and their hopes and fears for the future. This can result in the production of more balanced reports and, as a result, a fairer deal for the young offender.

The social enquiry report

Margaret Powell (1985) has noted that:

> The use of social enquiry reports in the sentencing process and the techniques adopted by probation officers in writing them produce many traps for the unwary. The criminal justice system, because it seeks to uphold the overall social and economic structure, is intent on identifying and dealing with offenders in terms of personal culpability. Social enquiry reports are an important part of this process of individualisation. . . . Because the courts respond to simple ideas and because the treadmill of writing reports saps the imagination, it is easy to for them to become cliché-ridden (pp. 27–8).

The problem of individualisation

We have already noted the importance of viewing individual delinquent acts in the context of structure, culture and biography. In doing this we are confronted with the paradox of the offender who chooses a course of action in a situation where, as a result of material constraints and socially and culturally given beliefs and attitudes, freedom of choice is severely limited.

As ideas go, this is not a particularly simple one to communicate. Yet if we are to avoid the trap, identified by Margaret Powell, in which we individualise what is essentially a social problem, communicate it we must. In doing this, however, we need to avoid the bland radicalism of 'society is to blame' and its equally vulgar conservative mirror image, that the offence was no more and no less than freely-chosen immorality.

This can be done much more easily in an SER if a shared 'language' and a set of shared assumptions is developed between the social, and IT, workers in an area and the juvenile court magistrates.

Jane's meetings

Jane is a project leader at an IT centre in the run-down inner ring of a large city. When she started at the centre she invited all the social workers to a series of meetings. She showed them a documentary made by some of the centre's clients. It was about the difficulties and temptations of growing up in the area. The film provoked a lot of discussion about the kinds of responses that social workers could make to problems which affected the whole neighbourhood. The social workers enjoyed the meetings, not least, they said, because they gave them a rare opportunity to talk and relax with each other. They said that one of the best things was that they were listened to and not just written off as people who locked up juvenile delinquents.

One of the outcomes of the meetings was that referrals to IT increased and recommendations of care and custody dropped sharply. Unfortunately the level of custodial sentences did not drop nearly as sharply and the social workers became very frustrated. They decided to devise a strategy for action at one of Jane's meetings. Somebody suggested that perhaps the magistrates could visit the IT centre. Jane agreed to explore the idea.

The magistrates duly arrived and Jane showed them the documentary the clients had made. The film provoked a lot of discussion about the kinds of responses that magistrates could make to problems which affected the whole neighbourhood. The magistrates enjoyed this, and the subsequent meetings which were arranged. They said that the meetings offered them a rare opportunity to talk and relax with each other. They said that one of the best things was that they were listened to and not just written off as people who locked up juvenile delinquents. One of the outcomes of the meetings was that commitals to IT increased and custodial sentencing dropped sharply.

In this example Jane's 'administrative' intervention effectively creates a place where a shared 'language' and a set of shared assumptions can be created and developed. This makes the job of the individual worker in the local juvenile court a great deal easier. One of the other spin-offs of this type of intervention is that magistrates who have had this kind of 'good' experience with workers from one authority will sometimes ask representatives of another to explain the lack of community alternatives to custody in their area. This, of course, does no harm whatsoever.

The attempt to put magistrates in touch with the realities of the lives of the young people who pass through their courts is an important one. If the defendant is over sixteen the SER might well contain an assessment of their chances of obtaining employment in the area and this can be supported by local job-centre statistics. An account of the local employment situation will not only inform magistrates, who usually live outside the area, of the realities of life there, but it may serve to modify their tendency to impose custodial sentences on unemployed young people more readily than they would on youngsters who are studying or in employment (Taylor, 1982 and Box and Hale, 1986).

The problem of the imprisonment

It would be hard, if not impossible, to think up an argument which demonstrated that imprisonment was in a young offender's best interest. It is more plausible to argue that imprisoning a young offender is in the interests of his potential victims, but here again the evidence suggests that imprisonment merely produces more serious offenders. Nonetheless imprisonment remains popular with politicians, newspapers and the public, and magistrates sometimes feel constrained to use it as a penalty in cases of violence or persistent property theft.

When contemplating imprisonment it is likely that considerations of deterrence and retribution will be at the forefront of the magistrate's mind and they are unlikely to be swayed by arguments which ignore these concerns and focus simply upon the needs of the offender. In this situation workers need to produce reports which explain why their recommended course of action constitute a more realistic and effective response to the offence than imprisonment. Such reports will usually be offence- rather than offender-focused, concentrating on how the worker plans to confront and deal with the offending behaviour. It is also particularly important, when a magistrate may be considering custody, that the SER offers an opinion about the relative impact of both custody and an alternative to custody, as is the case in the example below. The report should indicate the target of intervention, precisely what goals are to be achieved by the intervention and how long it will take to achieve these goals. One might write, for example:

Conclusion. *Clearly Gabriel's serious and persistent offending is causing concern to his mother, his teachers and his friends. Mr Tarkovsky, the educational psychologist, thinks that Gabriel is 'asking to be contained' and Mr Redford, his headmaster, has noted that Gabriel seems happiest when a member of staff confronts him with his misdemeanours and makes him behave properly. Gabriel can offer no explanation for his offending and when I first met him he seemed resigned to the inevitability of a youth custody sentence.*

As a result of his erratic childhood, and the extensive periods of time spent in residential care which resulted from it, Gabriel has become institutionalised. He finds it very hard to cope outside a residential institution and his mother, who is very depressed at present, cannot provide the structure he is seeking. He experiences all the disadvantages of youngsters leaving long-term care but because he has been able to return to live with his mother his problems have been masked.

In many ways a youth custody sentence would solve Gabriel's problems. Once offered the security of prison, however, he would probably want to keep coming back for more. At the moment he is a persistent offender but not a dangerous one. Unfortunately, somebody as uncertain of his identity as Gabriel could well be changed by the experience of imprisonment.

Recommendation. *In my view Gabriel needs much more structure in his life and a larger element of control. In addition he needs an opportunity to work on his identity. A one-year supervision order with a specified activity order attached could enable this to be achieved.*

Gabriel has been offered a place in the offending workshop at the Ford IT centre on two evenings a week for three months and I am proposing that this should be the activity specified by the court. The workshop will focus specifically on why he has offended in the past and how to avoid doing so in the future. I would attend three meetings with the project workers and Gabriel during this time to monitor his progress on the scheme. At the end of this period Ford will link Gabriel into their 'Big Brother' scheme and he will be paired with a volunteer who will engage in activities with Gabriel on some evenings and at weekends and act as an informal counsellor and befriender to him. I have, in addition, suggested to Gabriel that he consider joining the local NAYPIC group for young people leaving care and he has already attended it once. I would intend to see Gabriel on a weekly basis for the first three months of his supervision in order to support his participation in the offending workshop.

I would meet him fortnightly for the remaining nine months during which time I would intend to undertake counselling which would focus upon his confusion about his origins, his present identity and planning for the future.

I have discussed these proposed courses of action with Gabriel who is enthusiastic and prepared to commit himself to them should the court decide to offer him this opportunity.

The problem of the recommendation

The desire of social workers to find an effective means of intervening in the lives of young offenders sometimes results in the young person being pushed rapidly up the tariff of penalties and into a residential or custodial institution (cf. Thorpe *et al.*, 1980). The folklore of the juvenile court usually maintains that if a child who re-offends was previously given a supervision order then this time he or she should be sent to an attendance centre. In areas where this 'orthodoxy of escalation has been challenged the results, in terms of reconviction rates, are very heartening (Rutherford, 1986). These results can be achieved by not following the logic of escalation and making recommendations for disposals which are lower down the tariff 'Down-tariffing' may well break the pattern of a young person's system career. Young offenders carry the tariff in their heads and tend to accept the gradual worsening of their situation, seeing their eventual imprisonment as inevitable. As a result they come to feel fatalistic and this further erodes any incentive they might have had to stop offending. Wherever possible, the recommended disposal should aim to keep the young offender down-tariff because the movement up-tariff more often than not worsens the problem to which the court's disposal is supposed to be a solution.

There will be times however, when, because of the seriousness of the offence committed by a young person, magistrates will feel bound to impose a care order or a custodial sentence. However progressive our juvenile justice policies become, and whatever the ethics or effectiveness of institutional confinement, a few children and young people who commit particularly serious offences will continue to be locked up because we know of no other way to contain them. When we know that a child or young person faces institutionalisation we confront a choice. Do we leave it to the court to decide where the child should go, knowing that our silence will be read as unwillingness on the part of the local authority to assume responsibility, or do we attempt to pre-empt this decision by recommending a care order. As we have already noted, the introduction of the Children Act in 1991 will probably result in the substitution of the care order in juvenile criminal proceedings, for a new form of supervision order.) If we adopt the latter course of action we ask to assume parental rights and take on the responsibility for deciding whether to place the young person in a residential institution or not. The first course of action means a lot less work for the social worker and could be justified on the grounds that the young person sentenced to imprisonment has a greater degree of legal protection, in terms of the determinate sentence and the statutory entitlement to remission, than their counterpart who is 'sentenced to welfare' and whose destiny is determined by the social worker. On the other hand, knowing what we know about the negative impact of imprisonment on young people, we may decide that the young person's best interests are served if the decision about whether, when and in what type of institution he or she should be contained is taken by a social worker. This is not to argue that local authority residential establishments represent an ideal placement for a young offender, but rather that in a situation where the ideal response to serious, dangerous and persistent juvenile offending has yet to be invented, we seek out a response which minimises the chances of making a bad situation a great deal worse. Should imprisonment seem inevitable it may also be important to mention the young offender's need for education or treatment since this may have some bearing on whether or not he is sent to an establishment where these facilities are available.

The necessity of a positive and unequivocal recommendation to the court is underlined by research which indicates that where SERs contain no recommendation magistrates interpret this to mean that the social worker believes that the young person is beyond help in the community. De La Motta (1984) found that black defendants were the subjects of 'no recommendation' reports much more often than white defendants and this was an important factor in their disproportionate rate of imprisonment.

When a child or young person appears in court they are at a point of crisis, a crossroads, in their lives. As workers we encounter them at a point where they, and the social world they inhabit, are more open to change, for good or ill, than at almost any other time in their lives. If we can establish a purposeful relationship with them at this point then our future work with them will stand a much greater chance of success.

7

Direct Work with Young Offenders in the Community

Children and young people grow out of crime. Adolescents change, sometimes very fast. A new job, a new teacher, a new girlfriend or boyfriend, or just growing up and recognising the consequences of one's actions can make the difference. If we can hang on, and encourage other members of the network to hang on as well, then we can often see a child or young person through their offending and out the other side (Rutherford, 1986). It is within this situation of change and flux that we develop our face-to-face work with children and young people in trouble. Our responses to young offenders must reflect the reality of growth and change. The very different activities of playing Monopoly with a girl of 12½ and working with her as a young woman of 14 on the question of whether she should or should not embark upon a sexual relationship, are separated by a matter of months. We have to develop relationships in which youngsters feel free to be both children and adults without anxiety or shame. One of the most important things that adults can offer children and young people is a place where they can practice growing up while not having to be grown up.

Contracts

Whenever workers are working with clients a contract exists

between them. This contract may be implicit, as in the case of the duty social worker who offers a caller advice on welfare rights. No agreement has been signed but the caller knows he has a right to the advice and the worker recognises an obligation to give it. But in more fraught and ambiguous situations, as in work with young offenders, where the roles and relationships are complex and inclined to become confused, explicit contracts offer client and worker greater clarity in their transactions.

A contract is an agreement which specifies the rights and obligations of each of the parties to it. It states what rules exist, what the procedures will be if these rules are broken and the sanctions which can or will be involved. The contract specifies the roles to be played by the professional workers, the nature and extent of their authority and responsibility, and their accountability and confidentiality. It can state the frequency of meetings between the agent, the client and the activist and what will happen at these meetings.

The great advantage of the contract is that in the process of drawing it up each of the parties to it has an opportunity to negotiate its content and exert some control over what is eventually decided. This is particularly important for young people who have always experienced control as something imposed upon them from the outside and boundaries as things they discovered when they crashed into them.

This lack of experience in taking responsibility also means that workers should not encourage clients to enter a contract they will be unable to honour. If, in our anxiety to place clients, we steer them towards a situation in which they are unable to meet the demands, we are setting them up for failure. While the contract is notionally an agreement, freely and rationally entered into by all of the parties, on a basis of equality, and binding on each of them, we should not lose sight of the social reality that in an unequal society some people are in a better position to stick to a bargain than others.

In other words, a contract is a good thing to the extent that it offers greater clarity to all parties and a solid basis from which to work when problems arise. It is a good thing if it allows re-negotiation when experience proves that this is necessary. It is a good thing if it requires of the child or young person things that they will be able to achieve and value.

It is a bad thing if it is simply a recitation of what will happen to youngsters if they break the rules and offers no possibility for negotiation. It is a bad thing if it is devised only to assuage the fears and anxieties of adults. It is a bad thing if its expectations are out of line with a young person's abilities and allows him or her little opportunity to gain a sense of achievement. It is a bad thing if the young person experiences the contract as just another control or boundary imposed from the outside.

Working with individuals

Just as social workers cannot stop young people offending, they cannot 'solve' all of their problems either. Young people usually have to do this for themselves. If we can help them to solve their own problems then we are helping them to exert some control over, and make choices about, their own lives. If we can do this we have helped them to move from a situation they experience as acting upon them to one in which they are taking action in their own right, and to this extent we have helped them to gain a greater degree of independence and autonomy.

This is the primary objective of work with individuals, often referred to as counselling. Counselling is not necessarily best conducted in an office or in somebody's home. It is important to create an atmosphere in which young people can say what they want to say in their own way and in their own time. We need to be sensitive opportunists, using the environment imaginatively to create the right circumstances for counselling to take place.

It is important to try, as far as possible, to do what *feels* right. There is no instruction book to explain, when and how to engage a young person in counselling but we do have 'intuition', and we should listen to it and trust it.

We can create the right conditions for counselling if we engage in a shared activity. Children and young people sometimes think best and talk best when they are offered opportunities to stop talking, concentrate on something else or change the subject. This may be because they feel less trapped by the problem, or indeed the counsellor, if talking about the problem isn't the only option available or seems incidental to the activity. The counsellor for his or her part has to communicate that while it is fine to talk it is equally fine not to, and to do this without expressing it as indifference.

Most of the children and young people we work with will have more experience of talking about things than about feelings. As a result conversations that start from the concrete stand a greater chance of success. By and large people can deal with 'what?' questions better than 'why?' questions. 'Why' questions – 'why did you do this?', 'why did she say that?', 'why do you feel like this?' – are often experienced as persecutory. If we stick to 'what' questions – 'what did you do?', 'what did she say?', 'what do *you* feel?' – we will stay firmly within the experience of the client and the answers to the 'why?' questions will emerge anyway.

Sometimes children and young people find it easier to talk about the feelings and wishes of a hypothetical third party than about their own: 'what do you think boys like you would feel if this happened?', 'what do you think they'd want to do?' Like activity, this technique offers the client a degree of safety because it doesn't put them directly under the spotlight. It gives them a get-out, they can say what they really feel because they can always claim later that they weren't talking about themselves. With younger children, and this can sometimes include 10-year-old young offenders, the third person can be their favourite cuddly toy or cartoon character – 'What do you think Teddy thinks about this?', 'I bet She-ra would have something to say about that'.

On the basis of the information gained in the initial session or sessions we can help the client to define their need or difficulty more clearly, identify the choices which are open to them, and plan what they are going to do about it and how we are going to help them do it.

Our capacity to analyse and clarify may be the most important resource we can offer our clients. This conceptual reorganisation of the problem can help to transform the insoluble chaos the client was experiencing into a series of small achievable tasks and this may in consequence transform despair into optimism. We offer our analysis and clarification by summarising, paraphrasing and reflecting.

When we summarise we check with the client that we really have heard what they are trying to say. Our summary will inevitably be *our* understanding of what has been said. When we offer the client a summary we are not offering them what they said but what we *heard*. If we have listened carefully and sensitively, however, we will often find that we are giving them back what they really *meant* rather than what they actually *said*.

Paraphrasing allows us to identify the key themes in what is being said and offers the client and the worker a shared shorthand to use in talking about complicated situations. When we reflect back we hold up a mirror for the client to stand back and look at themselves. We offer them our understanding of what they have said to us in order that they can explore it further – 'do you mean you felt guilty?', 'it sounds like you don't actually like your boyfriend very much'. In doing this we use intuition to feel what it is like for the client and this is a perfectly proper way to work. It only becomes improper if we fail to check out the information supplied to us by our intuition with the client.

Individual counselling is a spiral. Our client speaks, we summarise, paraphrase and reflect. Together we define the problem and identify the components of a solution. We establish priorities and specify the tasks to be undertaken, who will do them and how they will be done. Together we evaluate how the tasks have been done and we offer the client feedback about their achievements in order to give them the strength and confidence to keep on with the next set of tasks. Faced with these tasks and an ever-changing situation our client speaks. We summarise, paraphrase, and reflect . . . until one day they don't need us anymore because through our work we have encouraged them to develop their own support systems and helped them to develop sufficient confidence and self-esteem to trust and rely upon themselves.

Working with friends

For many young people the transition from dependence to independence is supported by a small group of friends or one best friend. These relationships sometimes come to assume a greater significance than family relations and can last a lifetime. Interestingly, when young people are invited to attend an interview at a social worker's office they often arrive with a friend. This can pose a problem but it also presents an opportunity.

It may be that we will be able to engage the young offender more effectively if their friend becomes part of the interview. This sometimes helps to forestall the type of gruelling non-interview in which an increasingly desperate social worker tries to convey his or her message to a petrified, and hence effectively deafened, defendant.

Friends can help with the answers. Not being in trouble themselves, but often 'knowing the form' nonetheless, they tend to feel more relaxed and better able to ask the important questions which their friend who is 'on the spot' would not dare. They can also act as interpreters, often delivering our message far more succinctly than we are able. Our friends usually see us more realistically than we are able to see ourselves and recognise patterns in our behaviour of which we are barely aware. They can confront us with what we are doing more directly than any professional would dare, yet despite this, or possibly because of it, young people who apparently pay little or no attention to anybody else will listen to their friend.

Girls are more likely to associate with one or two, best friends than a larger peer group. Too often we have tried to shoehorn girls into fabricated peer groups of our own construction in the mistaken belief that we were reproducing the 'natural' milieu in which girls could be encouraged to get on with the developmental task. Men engaged in work with young offenders have often failed to ask, or listen to, female colleagues or girls. As a result we have missed some important information which has serious implications for our interventions. Girls are often much more able than boys to talk about their feelings and they tend to do this with their best friend. Sexism has prevented us from seeing the 'best friend' relationship as a target for intervention with young women in trouble. Marilyn Lawrence (1983) writes:

> 'When I first began working with young women, rather than adults, in a counselling context I was amazed at the ease with which 13 and 14-year-olds were able and prepared to talk to me. I had not expected their mature and thought-out understandings of their own social worlds, or the fact that they would be willing to share it' (p. 27).

She continues:

> 'I suspect that co-counselling has a great deal to offer. It is, after all, exactly what Best Friends, at their best, engage in anyway. It is also a powerful way of indicating that listening carefully to what other women

say, and in return, being listened to, is a proper and important activity. If twenty years of women's liberation hasn't taught us that it hasn't taught us anything' (pp. 28–9).

It is not that boys are never amenable to one-to-one or 'best friend' interventions. Many boys are not members of an identifiable peer group and are sometimes eager to discuss issues with a disinterested adult. It is rather that girls, by dint of socialisation, opportunity and a tendency to 'mature' earlier than boys, tend to be more responsive to interventions targeted at their thoughts and feelings about themselves.

Working with families

For effective family work to be possible certain conditions must obtain. It is necessary that family members, particularly parents, should be concerned about the 'problem'. There should be a fair level of agreement between the family and ourselves about the nature of the problem, and this 'problem' should fall within the terms of reference of our agency. Our client should still be an effective part of the family group and there should be some indication that family members have both a willingness and some ability to deal with things differently. We should be aware of whether the family has been offered family work before, whether or not they accepted it, and if they did, what the outcome was. We also need to consider whether or not we have the necessary skills to tackle all the potential levels of difficulty of the work.

Occasionally when we visit the home of a child or young person in trouble all of these conditions will obtain. We will meet a mother and a father who are eager to collaborate with our attempts to discover the cause and the remedy of their child's behaviour and who have both the desire and the capacity to confront the problems which may have led to their child's offending. More often, we will meet parents who are perplexed about their child's behaviour, ambivalent about our intervention, and uncertain about what, if anything, might be done about it.

Sometimes, however, we will meet parents who express no concern about the offence, our intervention or their child. This may be a consequence of depression, deprivation, or the despair which is induced by a life lived without hope, but whatever its cause it leaves us with a problem.

The most fully theorised area of social work practice is the family. If we encounter a family of the first or second type we have access to a substantial literature (some of which is cited in the Suggestions for Further Reading at the end of this book) and a wealth of practice wisdom upon which to draw. If, however, we encounter a family of the third type, then rather than working with the family we have to consider how we will be able to work despite it.

Working despite families

Young offenders who have 'uncooperative' parents tend to be punished for it. As in schooling, the child or young person whose parents appear interested in, and concerned about, their child's progress tend to be regarded by adult professionals as, at least potentially, interested and concerned themselves. Conversely, the children of parents who are reluctant to speak to social workers and loath to appear at court tend to be viewed as having a poor prognosis. Parental cooperation, or its absence, is regarded as a significant factor when welfare professionals are deciding whether a child or young person should be placed at home or in an institution. In court the attitude of the parents can make the difference between a custodial and a non-custodial sentence. There seems to be something fundamentally unjust about incarcerating youngsters in institutions because their parents aren't particularly interested in them. Indeed, it would accord more closely with the principles of natural justice if we incarcerated the parents and the social services department supplied the youngster with a full-time home help in order that they could stay at home.

If, in these circumstances, we wish to defend our client, and natural justice as well, we will have to ensure that any evaluation of the parents is not automatically and unthinkingly translated into assumptions about the child or young person. We will also need to develop a viable network of support which responds to the needs of, and offers a better self-image to, the child.

We may only ever be able to evoke grudging consent from the family for their child's involvement in this network and this is particularly so if the parents were themselves deprived as children. We all need to experience inclusion, affection and a sense of control over events. If the parents have been deprived in these areas and see their child having these needs met they may well become jealous. This might, of course, offer us a point of entry to the parents if we are prepared to respond to their needs as well, but it may also mean that the parents may attempt to sabotage the child's participation in the supportive network we have helped to construct. In these circumstances we may choose to use our authority to deflect the resentment away from the child and onto ourselves. We can tell the parents that the child is required, as a condition of his or her supervision, or care order, to comply with any directions we give them. In this way we may minimise the guilt and anxiety the child feels if they are enjoying themselves because we have told them that they have to do it. This *may* serve to protect them from being punished for their enjoyment, but it might not and we need to watch these situations carefully. This practice is by no means ideal but although we are working despite the family we are, paradoxically, still working with the family. Virginia Satir (1964) writes:

> However, concern with the family as a unit does not necessarily involve working with the whole family as a group, all the time. It is a focus for work, not necessarily a method of working. It simply means that, whatever is being done to help any member, the needs of the whole group, and the difficulties that any particular member has in meeting or reconciling himself/herself with these needs should be the primary focus.

We do not go through these elaborate contortions to keep the child in the community out of an irrational distaste for residential institutions but because research tells us that levels of offending often rise in the wake of a spell in care or custody, and that the removal of a child or young person from a problematic home for more than a few weeks makes it very difficult to replace them in it. This matters because even the best residential establishments for young offenders are seldom able to meet their emotional needs as well as what we might regard as very negligent families. We struggle to keep the child at home when we do, not because of an uncritical emotional or ethical devotion to the nuclear family, but because it is usually not as bad as the alternative and is, to that extent, 'good enough'. Apart from which, children tend to be tolerant, loving, and forgiving people who can make a lot out of the little they are sometimes given by their parents.

Working with natural groups

When we decide to work with natural groups we often do so because our client is hard to reach by other means. Alternatively, we may recognise that a young person's peer group is the most important source of positive influence in their lives or the milieu in which a lot of the trouble which they end up in, starts. Another, related, reason for intervention could be that the peer group, of which our client is a part, is causing concern amongst other people in the neighbourhood (Bright and Petterson, 1984).

Two British projects which targeted the natural group as their primary point of intervention were the Wincroft Youth Project and the Sheffield Detached Probation Project (Smith *et al.*, 1972; Hugman, 1974). Wincroft demonstrated that detached youth work offered an extremely effective method of reducing juvenile crime and custody in run-down inner city neighbourhoods. Sheffield proved that a neighbourhood approach which worked through existing friendship networks and peer groups allowed workers to make and sustain relationships with people who would never normally have gone anywhere near a social work agency.

More recently social workers and probation officers have instituted 'drop-in' evenings or obtained premises which they have used as 'drop-in' centres in an attempt to engage clients who are unresponsive in formal encounters. Work with the natural peer group is conducted on the client's ground and on the client's terms and raises once again questions of who exactly is the client and what is the target and purpose of our intervention. Social workers who have met their clients in cafés or pubs have often found that they have become *de facto* group workers with the client's peer group, some of whom are on their own or colleagues' caseloads, and some of whom, if only by the grace of god, are not. This is a situation where a golden opportunity to undertake purposeful and relevant work is in tension with the role confusion which could attend such work.

Because of these dilemmas, before we become too involved in

the natural group, we should clarify questions of accountability, responsibility and confidentiality with our client, his or her peers, our colleagues and our agency. For example, all parties will have to be clear about what is going to happen if we learn in the group that a colleague's client is truanting or involved in criminal activity. If the young people believe that confidentiality means keeping information we learn in the group to ourselves but we believe that it means confidentiality to the agency, then at some point our credibility in the group is going to be demolished and our relationship with our client seriously damaged. It is unlikely that we would have been introduced to our client's mates if he thought we were going to 'grass on them'.

Social workers caught in compromising situations like this sometimes say that, the client 'must have known that the information would be "passed on"'. In fact, many of our clients live in a world where if you are friendly with somebody, and they like you, and you like them, then you don't pass damaging information about them on to a third party who has the power to do them harm. If this happens it tends to be regarded as a betrayal. It is only social workers, probation officers and members of MI5 who don't abide by these rules. If these taken-for-granted rules are not the ones we are playing by then group members need to know this. We will not be rejected for being honest about the rules of the game but we will if we are seen to have implied one set of rules in our actions and then followed another.

Working with peer groups on their own ground and their own terms, because it removes most of the trappings of power and the props to professional identity, confronts social workers with questions about who they are, what they are, and what they have to give. Richard Pinder (1982), in an evaluation of attempts by probation officers to make informal contact with Afro-Caribbean young people, observed that as social workers we usually tend to deal *with* diversity in that we see ourselves as a social and cultural constant which confronts the ever-changing pageant of human diversity that trundles through our office. When we come out from behind our desks and enter the pageant, as we must if we work with the natural group, we have to start dealing *in* diversity which means that we have to open ourselves to the possibility that instead of being the person who changes a situation we might be changed by it. So it follows, ironically, that one of the most fruitful avenues of professional endeavour can also be the most threatening to professional identity. If, however, we are open to changing our ways of seeing, and being in, the world we may well find that the uncertainty which this engenders enriches our own lives and results in a better deal for our clients.

Working with formed groups

Workers form groups for young offenders in order to achieve one or more of three broad objectives, which we can characterise as *remedial*, *reciprocal*, and *social goals*.

Remedial groups aim to remedy or modify aspects of a client's behaviour perceived by the workers to be self-defeating, self-destructive, or threatening to other people. The 'remedy' may involve anything from psychotherapy to aversion therapy.

At present the major form of remedial group work with young offenders is to be found in the areas of the correctional curriculum (Thorpe *et al.*, 1980; Rutherford, 1986). The correctional curriculum endeavours to remedy delinquent behaviour by mobilising peer group pressure to modify group members' reactions to criminogenic situations. The groups operate upon the assumption that young offenders lack the necessary skills to effect law-abiding adaptations to the community in which they live. The workers use role play to enable youngsters to practice adaptive skills and abandon maladaptive ones.

> As with all social-skills training, the problem of application to real-life situations requires a lot of attention. The problem is how to generalise from the artificial group to the real world. In the case of learning new responses to sounding cues, it is helpful to produce as great a range of such cues as possible. Clearly this is done in the intermediate treatment group when the clients portray a wide variety of social situations antecedent to delinquency, and by means of role-play and discussion learn to discriminate between different anxiety-provoking stimuli. If it is the anxiety which produces the delinquent response (the outcome behaviour of particular stimuli), then face-saving formulae must be designed not so much to get the child out of the peer group, as to reduce anxiety (Thorpe *et al.*, 1980, pp. 147–8).

These groups in their pure form, aim to remedy particular behaviours by eradicating them and replacing them with others which enable active conformity to dominant social mores. To this extend a critical appreciation of the young offender as a critic of existing social arrangements, albeit an inarticulate and poorly focused one, tends to be edited out.

Remedial groups aim at quantifiable change in closely specified areas and tend, at points, to correspond to a medical model of intervention. The professional undertakes the diagnosis and prescribes the treatment. In reality, however, remedial groups of this type seldom exist in such a pure form, and reciprocal elements are either built in, or creep in.

Reciprocal groups aim to establish systems of mutual support. Group members in a similar predicament learn from, and help each other to deal with, survive in, or avoid, difficult, threatening, or stressful situations. Alcoholics Anonymous is probably the best known reciprocal group in the world. Many social workers run groups which enable children from chaotic and unsupportive families to teach each other their survival techniques.

In the 1980s the advent of consumerism in child care has seen the growth of reciprocal groups developed under the auspices of NAYPIC and Black and in Care. These groups are composed of, and run by, young people who have been in, or are on the point of leaving, residential care. Sometimes facilitated by adults, the groups aim to create a network of people in a shared predicament who can act as a source of mutual help, support and advice. The advantage of the reciprocal group is that by encouraging participants to be helpers as well as the helped it offers them more personal power and control than they would have in a remedial group or in a one-to-one relationship with a social worker.

The democratic banger racing project

Dave started a banger racing project. He believed that young people in trouble tended not to listen very hard to their social workers but that they took the opinions of their peers very seriously. Since they regarded the opinions of their peers as authoritative Dave decided to give the peer group authority.

As a result all decisions about who should come to the project, how they should behave when they were there, and what would happen if they re-offended while they were there, were made at meetings of the whole group. Dave insisted that if anybody's behaviour was causing anybody, adults or young people, concern then a meeting had to be called on the spot and the problem had to be sorted out there and then.

In response to a spate of offending by participants the group decided that if anybody re-offended they were out of the project. Dave said he thought this was 'a bit strong' but the group said that he didn't understand 'how these people's minds work'.

As a result of these draconian measures re-offending stopped and nobody in the group offended again during their time at the project. They talked a lot about it, and how to avoid it, but nobody did it.

Social Goals groups aim to bring people together to effect change in the world beyond the group. Tenants associations are the example, *par excellence*, of social goals groups and so are the local branches of NAYPIC in their campaigning role with local authorities. In the sphere of juvenile justice, social goals groups tend to be formed as part of administrative and political interventions (administrative and political interventions are dealt with in Chapter 10).

The role of the worker will vary according to the objectives to be achieved by the group. Workers in all types of formed groups occupy a central role at the beginning, not least because group members usually perceive the group as belonging to the worker. In the remedial group however, the worker tends to remain the 'central person' because he or she is the source and the repository of the remedy (Heap, 1964).

Workers in the reciprocal group may start as the 'central person' but they will aim to move to a position in the group from which they can enable group members to help one another. If the crucial difference between the role of the worker in the remedial and the reciprocal groups is missed it can lead to a great deal of confusion, particularly when a group has two workers with different perceptions of the worker's role.

In the *reciprocal* group the power and control which resides with the worker(s) in the early days of the group is gradually shifted onto group members. The objective here is the same as the objective to be achieved by counselling, namely that the group grows in competence and confidence to the point where it operates as an autonomous support system, and leaves its members with the confidence that they can solve their own problems and be instrumental in helping other people to solve theirs.

The worker in the *social goals* group is a resource who enables members to achieve goals which they specify. A NAYPIC Branch or a panel of professionals from the police, educational welfare, housing and social services convened to take action about high levels of custodial sentencing may need both a 'central person' at the beginning, and a 'facilitator' to help them through the interpersonal difficulties which may afflict them during their development. Ultimately however they will need a worker who can undertake background research on issues about which the group requires more information, service the committee, ensuring that what gets agreed gets done, and offer advice on strategy and tactics (Alinsky, 1972).

Withstanding the wind-up (a cautionary note)

As we have seen, the affront which some young people in trouble pose to those in authority is just as likely to seal their fate as their offending. We may well, as a result, find ourselves negotiating between the offender and powerful figures she or he has offended. When asked what has happened in these situations our client may, characteristically, reply that she or he was 'only winding the bloke up'. The 'wind-up' is one of the most effective tools available to young people in a relatively powerless position. It allows them to find out a great deal more about us than we would ever willingly reveal and so, in a situation in which we have a great deal 'on them', it gives them something 'on us'.

Like the tango, a successful wind-up requires two participants. It is a game which can only be played if both parties join in. Although it may not feel like it, the wind-up will only work if the intended target allows it to, because it is the target who holds the key to its success. The successful wind-up requires the target to take it personally. The moment they do this they are lost and the wind-up will begin in earnest. It is for this reason that workers with young people need to confront, and come to terms with, their own vulnerabilities.

If your ears stick out at right angles from the sides of your head but you don't mind, then adolescent humourists can spend days on end whistling the theme tune from Dumbo and it won't affect you, indeed it could become the kind of running joke that speaks of intimacy and affection. If on the other hand you reveal by your reaction that your ears have been the bane of your life, making you a pariah in the playground and a wallflower on the dance floor, you have offered your torturers the tool they need to chip away at your authority, and sufficient material to keep them in paroxysms of mirth for the forseeable future.

It is hard to overstate the importance for the professional worker of not taking hurtful personal remarks personally. They are seldom, in the first instance at least, directed at us because of who we are but rather because of what we are. Wind-ups are seldom malicious, they are designed as a test to see how far we will go, how much we will take and, importantly, whether, or not, we have a sense of humour. Children and young people often set considerable store by an adult's sense of humour and this is very astute of them because, as Norman St John Stevas once remarked, 'people with a sense of humour usually have a sense of proportion as well'.

The 'testing' of adults by adolescents is more less inevitable anyway, but people who have been deprived of the things they most need, as many of our clients have been, can be manipulative and exploitative. If they hadn't been, they might have got nothing at all instead of the precious little they did get. Like the rest of us they want, and as children they deserve, somebody to love them unconditionally and irrationally but they also know that the people who get close are in the best position to hurt them. In the resulting emotional mélange, harsh words are sometimes spoken and threats uttered but that is what we would expect from people who have every reason to be ambivalent about personal relationships. This is why we must confront our own vulnerability and ambivalence. With all of these contradictory emotions flying around it is important that we have a firm grip on our own so that we can remain the steady, predictable, unthreatening adults they need us to be.

8

Indirect Work with Young Offenders in the Community

Networking

Some of our clients have an unerring knack of getting themselves expelled, suspended, barred, banned, or otherwise ejected from all the schools, clubs, settlements, playgrounds, jobs, training schemes, social security offices, and pubs in their neighbourhood, and very often their own homes as well. This unfortunate tendency usually assumes the form of a crisis on or around 3.45 pm on a Friday afternoon. While it might be the case that a course of social skills training could avert such nastiness in the long term, faced with the prospect of yet another lost weekend, the worker will probably embark on some rapid networking.

Networking is a term which describes how workers with young offenders spend a lot of their time. It involves cultivating and supporting the minimum sufficient network necessary to sustain or contain the young person in the community. At the very least a child or young person needs a place to live, a person to ensure that they are eating regularly and a school to attend, if they are to remain outside of a custodial or residential institution. Networking is the process in which the social worker, or IT worker, acting as change agent, works indirectly with young offenders by mobilising and supporting the intricate nexus of people and agencies, the activists, which make a child or young person's survival in the community possible.

Lloyd Ohlin's observation that 'the total community experience of the youth before and after his correctional experience may overwhelm even the most constructive elements of the correctional programme' stresses the importance of effective networking (Ohlin, 1979).

The role of the worker

Schools, IT centres and Youth and Community projects will often be willing to offer opportunities to children and young people who have previously had difficulties if they know that they can count on the help and support of their social worker or IT worker. Their job is to underwrite the participation of a young offender by offering the activists in the network the security that if the situation becomes difficult they will intervene. Clearly this is a tall order but without such an assurance we may find it very difficult to enlist their cooperation.

It may well be the case that the difficulties our client experiences in an agency or organisation are, in part at least, a consequence of problems within it, rather than problems which they bring to it. In order to keep the network in working order workers need to address these problems. This type of intervention requires diplomacy but the task will be made somewhat easier if there is already in existence a contract which spells out the rights and obligations of the client, the change agent and the activist. The task will be made even easier however if the change agent has 'network credibility'.

Network credibility

It may not be a good thing but it remains the case that some social workers seem able to get exactly what they want from schools, courts and IT centres and some don't. Those who don't tend to dismiss those who do as lucky and in doing so betray a misunderstanding of how this oracle is worked.

We tend to get what we want if we have a good relationship with the person who is in a position to give it to us. If we arrive at the school 'cold' and start telling the teachers about how their school is failing to meet the needs of a young person who has dogged their days for the last four years this is unlikely to contribute to that good relationship. It is largely unjustified but not wholly surprising that some teachers and other professionals regard field social workers, to quote one of them as 'dilletantes who drift around pontificating about breast-feeding and potty training while every other bugger gets on with the work'. Such unfair stereotyping by other professionals is unfortunate for us but may have the more serious consequence of denying our client necessary resources to which they are entitled. This is why, in our work with resource-holders in the network we must develop *Network Credibility*.

Gaining credibility concerns gaining respect not sacrificing beliefs and principles. We can do this by doing our homework. Fellow professionals will take us more seriously if we know something about their job, the structure in which they work and the difficulties they encounter. We can find out about these things by visiting their school, adventure playground, club, IT centre or police station at times when we don't have a client that we want them to do something for, and talking to them and listening to what they have to say about themselves and their work. If we are known and accepted around the place then when we need to do business with them we are likely to get sympathetic treatment by dint of this familiarity. We don't have to agree with the people we meet, we don't even have to like them very much, but if they feel that we understand what they are trying to do and respect them, even though we don't necessarily agree with them, then they will usually cooperate with us. Social workers are not immune from the tendency to stereotype other professionals. Not all police officers are refugees from the third reich and not all teachers are authoritarian neurotics. We need to resist the tendency which leads us to feel morally superior to people whose point of view we have not tried to understand. Credibility is also about being reliable, predictable and honest. People who disagree with us or don't even like us that much will be able to work with us very easily if they feel that they can count on us.

Normalisation and informalism

Schools are normal and so are youth clubs and adventure playgrounds. Their great attraction is that, unlike specialist delinquency prevention programmes, everybody, whatever they have done, can go to them. If we can work with these normal resources we may be able to avoid a formal referral to specialist provision and so avert the stigmatisation which attaches to it. Formal involvement in delinquency prevention programmes may result in a young person attracting a heavier penalty at their next court appearance because this involvement fixes them in the minds of the bench and other professionals as 'delinquents' (cf. Thorpe *et al.*, 1980). A further risk of placement in specialist provision is that our clients may come to see themselves as so difficult, delinquent or dangerous that they have to be kept apart from normal people. The prejudice of others and their own negative self-image can be major factors in determining whether young people become seriously involved in crime or not. This is not to argue against specialist provision, but rather to argue for it to be used only when other, non-specialist, resources have been exhausted. We could well adopt the motto, KEEP IT NORMAL AND INFORMAL, when choosing the resources we are going to use. Youth and community work offers just such a range of normal and informal provision.

Youth and community work

Youth and community work embraces club and detached youth work, the work of adventure playgrounds and youth advisory or drop-in centres, community action campaigns with local tenants or residents groups, and community development work which assists local people to improve the resources in their neighbourhood.

Youth and community workers through their professional association have consistently resisted attempts by law and order governments, the social work profession and IT to implicate them in the statutory surveillance and control of young people in trouble. They have committed themselves instead to addressing the social, recreational and educational problems created for young people by poverty and a lack of access to opportunity and political influence (Robins and Cohen, 1978). This accounts in part for the dwindling fortunes of the youth service in a 'law and order' era. It is ironical that while the commitment of the youth service to informalism and normalisation would, on the face of it, make it an ideal resource for working with young offenders, governments in recent times have been too deafened by their own sabre-rattling rhetoric to realise this.

Youth and community workers have an implicit contract with the young people who use their premises and services which, were it to be articulated, would state that their first loyalty is to the young person and their best interests as defined by themselves. They have no contract with social workers or probation officers as agents of the court or the local authority. They have no obligation to share information with them and some very good reasons, in terms of their credibility with the young people with whom they work, not to. This is fine and it only stops being fine when workers in the juvenile justice system become confused about the different kind of relationship which they and the youth worker have with the young person.

The youth worker's role in relation to our client is to be somebody just for them, not for their parents, the magistrate, the local authority or the victim. In as much as any professional relationship can be, the relationship between the youth worker and the young person is uncompromised. The youth worker is paid, rather like the solicitor, to be partisan. This is what makes them important because, quite often, the youth worker will be the only person whom a youngster will trust, confide in and listen to. This means that we must handle our contact with them with great care in order that we do not compromise them in the eyes of the young person and so jeopardise this important relationship.

While it would be illegitimate to elicit information from youth workers it might be that by giving them information we can enable them to be more effective in keeping the young person out of trouble and in the community. If our client won't listen to us when we try to tell them about the likely consequences of their truancy, or failure to meet the requirements of a specified activity order, we might usefully communicate our fears to the youth worker who may be taken seriously because she or he may be seen by the young person as having no axe to grind.

Sometimes black young people will mistrust social workers, white and black, as agents of a juvenile justice apparatus which they regard, often quite correctly, as offering only discriminatory, 'white man's', justice and this can serve as a serious impediment to communication (Taylor, 1983). In this case, if we can communicate our concerns through a trusted youth and community, or adventure playground worker then we may be doing our client a considerable service. For this to work, however, we need to have established our credibility with these workers because by asking them to 'front' for us in this way we are asking them to put their own credibility on the line on our behalf.

It may at times be legitimate to let the youth, or community worker know something of our concerns about the client's family situation because he or she is likely to be the professional worker best placed to know about any informal support systems which exist, and those which could be created. They can also be instrumental in mobilising these indigenous support systems.

Whether, and to what extent, we should share confidential information with key professional or voluntary activists in a network, who would not otherwise have access to it, is a contentious issue. Clearly we cannot express concern without revealing something of its substance and yet, if we are expressing it to a voluntary worker in an informal local network, we may well be expressing it to a neighbour of our client's family. We should reveal as little as possible but beyond this lies the less certain terrain of our judgement and the intuitions and evidence we have about people's capacity for discretion.

In fact, of course, a lot of the time the issue is not how much we can tell them, because they already know and are concerned about the situation. The question is, how much can they reveal without 'dropping their neighbour in it with the authorities', namely ourselves? At this point it can be very useful if we acknowledge this concern and state as clearly as we are able what will happen to what types of information if they are revealed.

Because of their knowledge of the informal networks of relationships in neighbourhoods, youth and community workers can be key members of any inter-agency panel convened to consider crime and victimisation in the locality. It may fall to us as professional workers to explore with them the terms on which they might be persuaded to participate in such a venture.

The school

We usually become involved with the school if our client is either failing to attend it or behaving badly in it. Sometimes our role is to help the child or young person to negotiate their way back into it. This negotiation is important because teachers are sometimes not wholly displeased when a particular pupil fails to attend and if these teachers don't cooperate with the pupil's attempted 'come-back' it probably won't work.

We should discuss with our client what they do, and do not, like about school so that we can help them to articulate their view at a meeting with the school staff. At this meeting we will attempt to establish a 'contract' which covers questions of attendance, behaviour, procedures to be followed if difficulties arise which, if we are shrewd, will include a 'phone-call to us before anything irrevocable happens, and the programme to be pursued by the child or young person. Many schools are willing to construct special programmes to help reluctant pupils re-integrate into the school. These programmes build upon their strengths and de-emphasise those subjects or facets of school life which the youngsters find most difficult.

Most large comprehensive schools have a facility, variously described as a sanctuary, or a behavioural, off-site, or special unit. These units are designed to contain and work with children and young people who cannot cope with the usual school regime or with whom the usual school regime cannot cope. Considerable controversy has surrounded the creation of these units and the uses to which they have been put. Their critics call them 'sin bins' and argue that by 'dumping' its 'problem children' into specialised facilities the school is able to avoid confronting questions about the relevance of what it is offering to its most deprived pupils. Their defenders claim that special units are able to work creatively with children who would otherwise have been long-term truants or who would have been expelled from school. They say that the existence of special units frees classroom teachers to get on with the job of teaching pupils who want to learn while the children in the unit get the extra time and attention they require to fulfil their potential. In short, to the extent that the special unit merely serves as a mechanism for cooling out genuine dissent by problematising the complainants, it is a bad thing. To the extent that it brings specialised help to vulnerable children and young people who might otherwise have been lost to education it is a good thing.

We may reach a point with a client where their teachers are

saying that they no longer want them in the school and the child or young person is indicating by their actions that they don't want to be there either. At this point we may have to make a decision, or be part of one, about where to place the child. This is the point at which the *normal* and *informal* are exhausted and we find ourselves on the threshold of specialist provision. As we have already noted, whatever the intrinsic merits of the various specialist options available to us, there is an overarching question to be asked concerning the possible impact upon the client's 'system career' of any particular placement.

The regime and curriculum of an off-site unit administered by the local education authority (LEA) and of an IT centre administered by the social services department might be identical. The LEA might be nudging our client towards IT because their unit is oversubscribed and IT may have spare capacity. Even so we may still stick out for a place in the off-site unit in preference to IT because IT centres are places where juvenile criminals are sent and off-site units are places for children with learning or behavioural difficulties. Both are stigmatising but different stigmas have different consequences. While a placement in an off-site educational unit may serve to induct the child into a *special educational career* the end point of which is the residential special school, a child's progress through this system usually tends to be slower than their progress through the juvenile justice system. The stigma of a placement in an IT centre could result in the imposition of a heavier penalty when our client next appears in court because he or she is already in a delinquency prevention programme which, as their court appearance shows, has failed. Attendance at an off-site unit by contrast may be seen as evidence of a child's special needs which limit their culpability and commend them to the court as an appropriate object of its mercy. This illustrates the importance of finding out how the systems, into which our clients are likely to be inserted, operate at a local level. As we have seen, there is no single juvenile justice or special educational system and neighbouring areas may well operate in quite different ways. One of the things which is likely to vary most is the way in which Intermediate Treatment is used.

Intermediate treatment

Intermediate treatment has an identity problem. As a result of the ways in which successive government's have chosen to locate IT in their juvenile justice strategies its growth has both sporadic and theoretically and ideologically incoherent. This is one of the reasons why, all these years after the *Children in Trouble* White Paper (1968) which brought IT into being, workers and commentators are still unable to agree about what it ought to be.

At the core of this debate is the question of where IT should be located on the sentencing tariff and in the juvenile justice system. As we observed in Chapter 4, when we considered Nimrod's system career, IT can appear almost anywhere on the tariff, doing substantially different things to very different people, for profoundly different reasons. The minimalist critique of IT, articulated by Thorpe *et al.* (1980) and the Association of Juvenile Justice (AJJ), maintains that IT should only be used for diverting ajudicated offenders from care or custody. As we saw in Chapter 2 the main target of their assault has been 'preventive' work based upon the welfarist assumptions of the 1960s.

'Needology', they claim, is the assumption that a causal relationship exists between social deprivation and persistent delinquency and that it may be possible to prevent the latter by addressing the former (Thorpe *et al.*, 1980). The critique maintains that by encouraging the participation in IT of youngsters who are 'at risk' of, rather than actively involved in, juvenile crime we inadvertently propel them deeper into the juvenile justice system. In inducting them into a 'preventive' group we establish them in their own minds and in the minds of magistrates and welfare professionals who will subsequently meet them, or read their files, as 'delinquent'.

This is seen to have three related consequences. First, having been officially labelled as 'delinquent' by dint of their participation in a group for people at risk of delinquency the child may well proceed to take on the deviant label and act it out by becoming 'delinquent'. Second, because the child is officially established as 'delinquent', courts and welfare professionals will regard any offence they might subsequently commit as symptomatic of a deviant behavioural pattern or pathology rather than an isolated incident or a normal part of growing up. This will result in the imposition of more serious penalties or more intensive and lengthy treatments in an attempt to arrest the anticipated decline into serious and persistent offending. Third, because the child has already 'had' IT prior to committing their first offence, when they do, they enter the juvenile justice tariff a few rungs higher up than a child who is equally deprived but unknown to social workers.

Although the minimalists offer us little empirical evidence of these processes at work their argument is plausible and coincides with observations which workers in the juvenile justice system sometimes make. They alert us to the problem, identified already in this book, that benign intentions can have malignant consequences.

One obvious reservation we must raise however is that in the typical British urban social services district where even cases of non-accidental injury remain unallocated there probably aren't many people doing preventive group work with 'pre-delinquents' any more. Since it is this work which is often cited as the primary cause of net-widening in the juvenile justice system, we might assume that the central problem raised by the minimalists has, to a large extent, been answered, if only by default.

While their criticisms of pre-emptive intervention are important the minimalists have muddied the waters by presenting the central problem confronting the juvenile justice system as that of the unintended consequences of social work intervention. Their insistence on the superiority of minimal or non-intervention in all circumstances has served to polarise the debate around the question of *Intervention versus Non-Intervention*. As a result we are discouraged from considering critically the quality of any particular intervention. The graphic instances of inept practice presented by the minimalists are never constrasted with the innumerable instances in which sensitive counselling and politically astute advocacy by social workers and IT workers, at all stages in a young person's system career, have had highly creative pay-offs.

What the minimalists fail to understand is that social work has learnt a lot from them and as a result many practitioners frame their interventions with an eye to their possible unintended consequences. The message about moral contamination has got through and so has the one about the strategic use of IT to de-escalate a young person's career.

Clearly, any attempt to characterise the different forms which IT takes and the purposes it pursues is unlikely to meet the objections of all the protagonists in this debate. It is true to say, however, that most IT provision falls into the following categories:

1. Low-intensity individual prevention
2. Low-intensity social prevention
3. Low-intensity alternatives to prosecution
4. High-intensity alternatives to care or custody

Number 4 can be further subdivided into:

i. High intensity day-care
ii. Strategic alternatives to your custody

1. Low-intensity individual prevention

Low-intensity individual prevention locates the client as the target for intervention and aims to control and prevent their present and future offending. This intervention often takes the form of a one-night-a-week group for younger offenders or 'pre-delinquents' whose involvement in crime is either slight or non-existent but who are considered to be 'at risk' because of their family's present circumstances or history. Characteristically these low-intensity groups are composed of boys and girls aged between 10 and 14 years whose brothers and sisters are, or have been, in trouble with the law and whose parents have been unable to prevent this or support their children through it. Groups like this attempt to offer the children support, 'compensatory' positive relationships with adults, and a measure of control over some aspects of their lives. They aim to help the children develop their powers of self-control and a capacity to exert choice about their own behaviour. They are useful places for children who are confused about boundaries. The workers often attempt to engage the group in an exploration of these boundaries by identifying the social skills group members will need to survive at home and at school. In addition the programme usually includes trips out, camping weekends and holidays. The low-intensity group does what generations of social workers have done with deprived and impoverished children. In attempting to transmit survival skills and project the children into new and pleasurable activities workers attempt to compensate the children for their deprivation.

As professional users of IT we must be aware of the likely impact of any given intervention on a young person's system career. It is not that clients who are deprived and on the fringes of crime should never be involved in preventive groups but rather that before we refer a client to a group we are clear about how we will deal with the fact of their participation at any subsequent court appearance. As a rule of thumb, if the child's participation is voluntary and not a condition of a court order or an agreement made with a magistrate, then the contract is between the child, the group workers and the social worker. In this case such participation is, quite literally, no business of the court and if it seems likely that mention of such participation might prejudice the court's view of the child then it is best omitted.

2. *Low-intensity social prevention*

Low-intensity social prevention locates the client as the target for intervention but it also aims to fulfill an implicit contract with the neighbourhood which is the actual and potential victim of juvenile offending. It is an intervention geared to changing the behaviour of an aggregate of children and young people rather than the personal or interpersonal behaviour of particular children and young people.

In the mid-1970s the police in a London borough noticed that the juvenile crime rate in that traditionally crime-prone district dropped during the school summer holidays and rose again during term time. The drop was attributed to the extensive and highly successful summer playschemes developed by voluntary and statutory youth service agencies in the borough. This is all the more remarkable because the summer holidays in most inner-city areas are periods when the incidence of recorded juvenile crime usually rises. As we have seen, what happened in London in the 1970s was replicated in France in the 1980s.

Social prevention is based on the idea that by engaging children and young people who live in crime-prone neighbourhoods in social, educational, recreational or political activities it may be possible to divert them from crime. Social prevention strategies tend to be unselective assuming that in opening their doors to everybody in the age range they will inevitably make contact with a substantial proportion of deprived and actually or potentially offending children and young people.

Whereas some IT sections still run social prevention projects in the form of summer playschemes and provide resources like hobbies workshops which are open to all the children and young people in crime-prone neighbourhoods on demand, the contemporary critique frowns upon such unfocused, 'shotgun', responses to young offenders. Its critics claim that social prevention is, by and large, just 'needology' on a broader canvas. It is, they say, theoretically dubious because it views the phenomenon of juvenile crime as the product of juvenile offenders rather than as a consequence of the interaction between the child and the agents of the juvenile justice apparatus. They argue that rather than dissipating resources on poorly-focused social prevention programmes we should invest them instead in high-intensity alternatives to care or custody. What these critics ignore are the quantifiable benefits of such programmes for the potential victims of juvenile crime and the possibility that it might be beneficial for children to be diverted away from crime itself and not just the juvenile justice system. Both the Wincroft Youth Project and the Massachusetts Experiment, cited earlier, produced evidence that social prevention can reduce juvenile crime rates. One of the other great advantages of social prevention for social workers looking for the least stigmatising community placement for a client is that although these projects are concerned with offenders and offending the young person's involvement remains normal and informal.

3. *Low-intensity alternatives to prosecution*

Whereas low-intensity alternatives to prosecution usually require the young offender to do *something*, the primary target for change is the behaviour of police officers. The intervention aims to persuade the police not to initiate a prosecution and to issue a formal caution or take 'no further action' against a child or young person instead. In order to encourage the police to act in this way voluntary and statutory agencies, and sometimes the police themselves, have initiated (front-end) diversion schemes. These schemes offer to engage young offenders, and sometimes their families as well, in social, recreational or educational activities if the police will agree not to refer the case to the Crown Prosecution Service.

Where front-end diversion schemes operate they are reliant upon the good will of the police, who agree not to exercise the powers available to them, and the commitment of the statutory and voluntary organisations which provide the diversionary back-up.

It is important to recognise that while one of t' , stated aims of front-end diversion schemes may be the prevention of further offending, their major purpose is strategic. They aim to do 'less harm' rather than 'more good'. They attempt to avert the damage wrought by projecting a child or young person into a 'system-career'. They are based on the, largely correct, assumption that while most children and young people are, from time to time, involved in offending, the overwhelming majority of them grow out of it and that they will be much more likely to grow out of it if we haven't slapped a 'delinquent' label on them and spoiled their identities. Front-end diversion schemes are concerned to promote tolerance rather than eradicate deviance and this can be very helpful to young people in trouble.

4. *High-intensity alternatives to care or custody*

(i) High-intensity day-care. IT Day care is provided for the minority of young offenders who are unable to survive in the schools, clubs and play facilities available to other children, but whose predicament would be worsened by incarceration.

Day-care developed as the dominant model of intensive IT in the mid- to late 1970s. Implicit in this development was the assumption that persistent juvenile offenders needed continual support and surveillance. What became clear as IT day-care got into its stride was that while this assumption held true for some of them, many were perfectly able to survive outside of what was in effect an institution.

Day-care straddles the border between the residential establishment and the community. It tends to be used for both children at risk of reception into residential care and for those placed temporarily with foster parents or in childrens homes. For the former group, day-care offers an alternative to the institution which responds to their needs but avoids the more disabling side-effects of induction into a total institution. For the latter group, day-care offers the possibility of maintaining links with their community when, because of recurrent family crises, they are temporarily unable to live at home.

The target for day-care intervention is first and foremost the child or young person, their needs and the quality of the relationships they are able to sustain in the community. Day-care offers a sheltered, 'greenhouse', environment to vulnerable children and young people in which they are offered opportunities to develop the skills and attributes they will need to be able to survive outside an institution.

(ii) Strategic alternatives to youth custody (YC). Unlike day-care, which attempts to maintain or modify the behaviour of children and young people in trouble, strategic alternatives to YC aim to maintain or modify the behaviour of the juvenile bench. Strategic alternatives may contain educational, recreational, and work-experience elements but at their core is a 'correctional' component which, their advocates contend, is its major selling point to hard-bitten juvenile magistrates who want to see a response to juvenile crime and not just the needs of juvenile criminals. Strategic alternative 'packages' are tailored to the demands of the court and attempt to anticipate and reflect the type and duration of the sentence a young offender will attract. The 'correctional' component in the package may include participation in a victim and offender scheme, reparation, community service and participation in an offencing workshop which operates a 'correctional curriculum' of the type discussed in Chapter 7.

It is only after these specialist community-based resources have been exhausted that the young offender should enter an institution. As we shall see, however, this is not always the case.

9

Working with Young Offenders in Care and Custody

Residential care

Removing a child or young person from their own home is usually difficult and painful for them, their parents and the social worker who has to do it. This is one of the least palatable parts of a social worker's job and one which requires a great deal of thought and sensitivity. For this reason it is important to address the ways in which these removals can be minimised and the mechanisms whereby the large numbers of children and young people who should not be in care or custody get there.

Care orders may be imposed as a result of a social worker's recommendation but they are sometimes imposed despite it, in circumstances in which a supervision order would offer the worker adequate powers of intervention. It is for this reason that reformers have supported the proposal in the Children Bill 1989 to substitute the care order in juvenile criminal proceedings with a new form of supervision order which gives the local authority less power. Magistrates sometimes argue that they are forced to impose care orders because they know that in times of staff shortages and cut-backs, supervision orders receive a low priority, often remaining, actually or effectively, unallocated for the duration of the order. The danger inherent in this practice is of course that it moves the young person up-tariff, making him or her vulnerable to future incarceration.

If a young person who is the subject of a care order but placed 'at home on trial' reappears in court, magistrates may, out of frustration at the local authority's apparent inaction in the case, impose a custodial sentence. This is done in order to punish the defendant but also to get the social services department and social workers to 'buck up their ideas up'. It is not unknown for young offenders to be caught in the crossfire of conflict between a juvenile bench and a Social Services Department, over the alleged failure of social workers to respond adequately to the wishes of the court.

This escalation of penalties as a response to dwindling social work resources is an important mechanism whereby children and young people are inducted into care and custody and points to the importance of departmental systems management strategies, and liaison with the juvenile bench, to counter this tendency. The case for these strategies is strengthened when we consider the available evidence about the ways in which social workers use care orders.

Thorpe *et al.* (1980) in their analysis of children and young people admitted to CHEs cite the 'care and control' test which specifies the three criteria, one or more of which should obtain, before a young offender is removed from home and placed in a residential establishment. They are:

1. That the child is a danger to himself and/or the community.
2. That the child does not have a home in the community which can, with appropriate support, provide an adequate degree of care and control.
3. That the child has specific medical, educational, vocational, or psychiatric needs which can be dealt with only in a residential context (pp. 80–1).

Given the range of resources and methods of intervention available to us there should, if these criteria were adhered to, be very few circumstances in which it would be necessary to take young offenders into residential care. However, Thorpe *et al.* found that between 70.5 per cent and 90 per cent of CHE placements were inappropriate in terms of these criteria and this raises the question of why social workers were so keen to incarcerate young offenders.

One common reason for seeking a residential placement is that the social worker doesn't know what else to do. Millham *et al.* (1978) and Cawson and Martell (1979) have noted that a substantial number of the youngsters admitted to secure units were there as a response to the administrative and resource problems of social services departments rather than problems generated by their own 'pathologies'. We have to remember that just because we've run out of ideas, and probably patience as well, it doesn't mean that other workers, workers in statutory and voluntary IT programmes, youth workers, teachers, clergymen, or the owner of the café our client and his friends frequent, have as well. Sometimes a little humility and a willingness to admit that we don't have the answer can prevent a difficult youngster from being projected even deeper into a deviant career.

Another reason why some young people wind up in a CHE is that their social worker has threatened that if they keep on doing whatever it is they are not supposed to, they will be removed from home. The problem with threats is that they limit our room for manoeuvre and negotiation and leave us feeling stupid if we don't act on them when our bluff is called. Locking up a child or young person so that we don't look silly doesn't have anything to do with social work but it has a lot to do with our own insecurities.

Social workers often find themselves under pressure from magistrates, parents or other professionals to 'do something' about a child or young person in circumstances where there is nothing useful to be done. This pressure is at its most acute when an adolescent is exhausting the patience, or posing an affront to the authority, of an adult. Sometimes the most problematic feature of a situation can be the frustration of anxiety of other adults who deal with their feelings by trying to pressurise the social worker into precipitate action. The ensuing action may well assuage the frustrations and anxieties of the adults but it is unlikely to serve the best interests of the child. Our role in these circumstances is to work with the feelings of the adults in the situation, not to remove the child or young person from it.

Sometimes social workers will try to get a care order under the offence condition of the 1969 CYPA because they don't have enough evidence to get one under another section of the Act. The recent spate of public enquiries into the role of social workers in cases where parents have murdered their children points to the difficulties social workers face in amassing sufficient evidence even to remove a child from a life-threatening situation. Nonetheless, by using the offence condition as a device to remove a child or young person from an unsatisfactory home we run the very serious risk of inducting them into a deviant career by moving them so far up-tariff while simultaneously, and quite literally, taking liberties away from the parents and the child. The 'delinquent' label also makes these children and young people harder to foster and this abuse of the Act, however well-intentioned, is seldom if every justifiable.

It seems unlikely that the introduction of a new (residential) supervision order in the Children Act, due to be implemented in 1991, will, of itself, lessen the pressures on social workers to remove young offenders from their own homes. While it may well limit the power of the local authority, it will do nothing to limit the power of juvenile court magistrates, provide adequate alternatives to care and custody, create juvenile justice policies within local authorities, institute systems monitoring procedures and reduce social workers caseloads. Unless these other factors are addressed it is likely that we will continue to remove more juvenile offenders from their homes than virtually any other European country.

Some social workers actually place young offenders in residential establishments for young offenders in order to eradicate their offending. Cornish and Clarke (1975) cast serious doubt upon the efficacy of this endeavour. Their study shows that while detected offending was marginally reduced while a child or young person was in a residential establishment, it reverted to its former level upon their release. Michael Zander (1974) suggested that rates of offending actually rose as a result of placements in residential establishments. Much of this additional, and often more serious, offending tended to occur when youngsters absconded from establishments and attempted to make their way home. What does seem clear from research and the observations of workers within the juvenile justice system is that residential 'treatment' of delinquency has few if any beneficial long-term effects and often tends instead to make matters considerably worse.

Receiving a young offender into care

Probably the most important thing that we should be considering when we take young offenders away from home is when we are going to take them back again. Research commissioned by the DHSS (1987) indicates that what happens during the first six weeks in care will determine the shape of a child or young person's system career, possibly for years afterwards.

A clear 'care plan' which charts the when, where, who and how of the youngster's re-integration into the family if this is possible, or long-term placement plans if it is not, is crucial. If a child or young person is removed from a problematic family for more than a few months then the 'wound' left by their removal heals over, and it becomes exceptionally difficult to reintegrate them into it. This suggests the importance we should place on regular contact between youngsters and their families and the proximity of the residential establishment or foster placement to their homes. If they can, for example, have their evening meal at home two or three times a week and spend Sundays with their families then it is much more likely that places will, as it were, be kept for them.

Adolescents form the bulk of the long-term care population. When they tell us that their parents really do want them at home but there isn't enough room because of all the younger children, or that mum and dad are going to send for them any day now, the feeling of abandonment and the desperate need to hold on to the fantasy of being wanted are palpable. Though less obviously dependent on their families than younger children, and even though they might be in conflict with their parents, they badly need a family to re-enter. Our job in this situation is to so organise things between the child or young person, the parents and brothers and sisters, and the residential home or foster-parents, that families which have difficulty with the mechanics of caring, or don't actually care very much, are enabled to express that care to the child or young person as regularly and as often as possible. Sometimes, the maintenance of affectional bonds presents itself to us as an organisational problem.

If social workers have been unable to create and operationalise an effective care-plan within the first six weeks after a reception into care they sometimes lose interest, things start to drift and the youngster can be effectively abandoned within the care system (DHSS, 1987). The immediate pressure of the reception into care is off, things feel as if they have settled down and other, more urgent, cases or crises interpose themselves between the social worker and the young offender. This feeling of calm after the storm should serve as a warning to social workers that they are losing their grip on the situation.

Social workers sometimes experience the reception of one of their clients into care as a personal defeat. If they have tried as hard as they can to keep a young person in the community they may feel guilty, believing that they have let their client down. They may also feel embarrassed that they did not have adequate professional skills to keep the child out of an institution. What they will find harder to admit is that they may also feel angry towards the client who has made them fail and the staff of the residential establishment who are witnesses to that failure and who appear to be dealing with the client competently.

These feelings are both understandable and common and they only become damaging if they remain unacknowledged and are acted out. One of the reasons field social workers sometimes 'abandon' clients in residential care or express an irrational antipathy towards, or about, the staff of residential establishments is that they have not come to terms with the guilt, sadness and sense of failure which can be induced when we run out of ways of sustaining a child or young person in the community. We have to acknowledge that 'we can't win them all'. We have to forgive ourselves for not knowing everything and not being able to do everything. We have to do this because if we can accept ourselves as ordinary people trying to do our best in a difficult situation, then our fantasies and frustrations about our own omnipotence and infallibility won't stand in the way of our client getting the best possible service from us.

Custody

With the implementation of the 1982 CJA the prisons finally abandoned their rehabilitative pretensions. From this point onwards the British penal system offered the young offender imprisonment pure and simple. This was a significant shift for those social workers who had sometimes been tempted to recommend custody for intransigent clients. They had reasoned that while Borstal might, or might not, serve as a salutary lesson, the trade training it offered was second to none and equipped youngsters to make a living as plumbers and electricians. Who, they reasoned, would bother to resort to crime when they could ligitimately charge a £65 call-out fee to turn off somebody's stopcock?

Young offender institutions offer neither rehabilitation nor training. As evidence of their apalling reconviction rates, and assaults upon, and violations of the civil rights of, inmates are revealed, it becomes clear that if there ever was a time when custodial confinement could be justified in terms of the best interest of the young offender, those days are over. In the 1980s, partly as a result of demographic changes, the actual numbers of juveniles entering the juvenile justice system and penal establishments dropped. It was also the case however that those youngsters who were caught up in the system were more likely to be imprisoned and to serve longer sentences: 'Between 1970 and 1985 the proportion of boys aged 14 to 16 convicted of indictable offences who were given a custodial sentence rose from 6% to 12%. For girls the rise was from under 1% to over 2%. There was also a move towards the longer youth custody sentence and away from the shorter detention centre order' (NACRO, p. 11, 1987).

The young offender institutions which replaced the DC and the YCC in 1988 are prisons and as such they are heir to all those features of total institutions which, Goffmann (1968) suggests, conspire to 'spoil' identities. The central irony of imprisonment is that it brings together large numbers of people who have nothing in common but crime and offers them almost limitless time and opportunity in which to discuss, boast about and fantasise upon it. Not surprisingly when inmates finally leave prison they find it very hard to think or talk about anything but crime and prisons. Thus it is that the experience of imprisonment may serve to recast the identity of a young person into that of a 'prisoner'.

Nigel Stone (1985) suggests that in our work with people in prison we need to address the related issues of identity and survival. This starts in the custody room or cell after the judge or magistrate has passed sentence. It will probably be the social worker who takes a young person's family or friends there to see them. This is, inevitably, a fraught situation where sadness is mixed with anger, and the safest person upon whom that anger can be vented may be the worker. 'Why did you say this?', 'Why didn't you say that?', and 'You fitted me up' are hard for us to hear when we have worked hard to forestall imprisonment but people who have just been sentenced don't usually want a reasoned argument.

What they need is somebody who is strong enough to sit and listen while they express their anger and fear. Sometimes a young person will be under a lot of pressure to put a brave face on it in order to protect his mother and father or brothers and sisters from the pain of separation. In this case the social worker may be the only person to whom the youngster can express the fear, loneliness and sense of loss. We should remember that the first custodial sentence may also be the first time that a young person is going away from home and this can be difficult even if they are going somewhere they want to be.

We can listen and assure our client of our continuing interest in them. We can assure them that we will inform everybody they want informed about where they are and how they can be contacted. We can tell them that we will stay in touch with their family to see that they are 'alright'. And we can imply, if it is appropriate, that we will encourage a family, which might not otherwise be very good at it, to write and visit. Getting this to happen is very important because, as we have seen, part of our job is to ensure that the young person has an emotional and geographical place to come back to when they are released.

For our own part we need to get our diaries out and plan our future visits and letters. We should also mark the young person's birthday and make a note a few days before this date to send them a card and possibly a small present as well. We should add their name to our Christmas card list. This may sound trivial and somewhat mechanistic, but emotional survival in prison is, in large part, constructed out of letters and visits. If there is somebody on the outside who cares enough about you to remember you on your birthday and at Christmas then you might possibly be more than just another 'prisoner'.

There are no guarantees that our client will be placed somewhere accessible to their family and friends. The families of most of the people in prison are poor. They often have no car and cannot afford to spend a great deal of money on public transport. In this case the best interest of our client are served if we can either drive family or friends to the prison or procure the fare so that they can travel on public transport. Maximising contact in this way maximises opportunities to be somebody other than a prisoner and it reminds young people of who they have been and who they can be again.

Throughcare

The 1982 CJA reduced the period of statutory aftercare for young people leaving penal establishments and in doing so indicated that the government placed a low priority on aftercare and throughcare. This downgrading is reflected in the metamorphosis of the 'Probation and Aftercare Service' into the 'Probation Service' in 1983. This changed identity is reflected in the low priority the service has given to throughcare in the wake of the Act. Paradoxically, while the Act served to lessen the commitment of the probation service to aftercare the local authority social worker was handed a new set of statutory throughcare responsibilities.

Many young people, and not a few professional workers, regard statutory post-release supervision as an impediment to beneficial contact rather than a mechanism which facilitates it. Young people often feel that they have 'done their time' and see the requirement to report regularly to a social worker or probation officer as an illegitimate incursion into their freedom and privacy. Supervising officers for their part will often argue that the conditions of supervision generate such suspicion and anxiety and so emphasise the differential power of the social worker and the client that any contract or agreement between them must inevitably be something of a sham. As a result very few people are ever prosecuted for non-compliance with the requirements of a licence.

In an attempt to make aftercare more relevant and workable some young offenders teams in probation, social services departments and IT have developed drop-in facilities where young people who have been released from prison can come for information and advice on jobs, training, education or more personal matters. They can just drop in and talk with whichever member of the team they wish. Some young people don't 'drop-in' but non-reporting appears to be less of a problem in this set-up than in offices which have stuck to a more traditional model of licence supervision. Indeed if the drop-in model has a problem of attendance it is that some young people find it such a supportive milieu that they become loath to go out into the cold hard world in pursuit of the few jobs available to youngsters who have been in prison.

Realistic aftercare which responds to the needs and interests of young offenders, as distinct from the statutory surveillance and control envisaged in the 1982 CJA, is a pressing necessity if a young person's first experiences of care or custody is not to serve as an entrée to an institutional career.

Preventing care and custody

It sometimes seems that a child or young person is 'asking to get caught'. While this behaviour may be a way of testing out adults or acting out a problem it may also be exactly what it appears to be, a request to be caught.

Some young people try to get caught and 'put away' because this feels better to them than 'freedom'. Saul Bellow says that we must either organise our freedom or drown in it and a lot of our young clients are in grave danger of drowning in it. A freedom which requires a young person to be alone in a cold flat with the dole money spent and the heat and light cut off compares unfavourably with a captivity which allows him to play pool in a warm association hall after a hot dinner. In these circumstances our job is to help young people to find something worth staying out for.

The prison and the CHE can meet the dependency needs of deprived and isolated children and young people. The irony of emotional deprivation is that instead of equipping those so deprived with an enhanced capacity for independent living, it intensifies their desire for dependency while diminishing their ability to cope with the intimacy which dependency entails. The prison and the CHE go to considerable pains to ensure that inmates depend upon them, they meet a young person's material needs and protect them from the anxiety and uncertainty of freedom. Unlike other dependent relationships, these institutions do not offer intimacy and so they are perfect for young people who fear both intimacy and freedom. In these circumstances our job is to help young people to transfer their dependency from the institution and to begin to consider the consequences of their drastic attempts to get their needs met.

Whether we are dealing with young people who have no reason to stay on the outside or those attracted by the vestigal emotional solace on offer inside, we need to address the ways in which we can work with our clients to develop both the support systems and the skills which are necessary for survival outside of an institution. The

1980s witnessed the emergence of schemes and projects designed to help youngsters leaving institutional care. Their initial concentration upon practical skills is now complemented by work which focuses upon identity. These shifts have been promoted in part by consumer organisations like NAYPIC and Black and In Care and they have drawn our attention to the need for continuing support in developing a non-institutional identity and a network of friends and contacts for young people leaving care. Our task is to help them develop a network in which both material needs and the emotional need for inclusion, affection and a sense of control over one's own life may be met.

For young people leaving care or custody the prospects are bleak. They often find themselves pushed to one side in the competition for employment and housing. Children and young people returning to their neighbourhoods from care and custody need an advocate who will champion their cause in the places where decisions are made about the allocation of scarce resources and opportunities. This requires political intervention in local agencies and local government itself. If social workers, probation officers or IT workers are unwilling to do this it is unlikely that anybody else will.

Dealing with abuses

Institutions which run smoothly sometimes do so because an implicit or explicit deal has been struck between the staff and high status members of the informal inmate pecking order. In these circumstances it becomes very important that a young person doesn't get on the wrong side of either group because this can mean living with the consequent victimisation (Mathiesen, 1964).

Prisoners say that 'inside you have no friends' by which they mean that in this dangerous world inmates can seldom afford to trust each other because 'grassing' is rife. They will seldom if ever support each other in disputes with staff or powerful inmates. To do so would be to violate the injuction, subscribed to by prison officers and inmates alike, which enjoins each prisoner to 'do your bird'. 'Doing your bird' involves not complaining about being inside, denying any feelings you might have about it, and accepting the routine injustices of prison life with stoicism. 'Doing your bird' is also a psychological mechanism whereby feelings of sadness and loss are avoided by focusing on the here and now of the prison routine and engaging only in 'prison talk'. Young people who become immersed in prison life do so in large part because it is less painful than thinking, or talking, about what happened and is happening on the outside (Cohen and Taylor, 1980).

As social workers we may be the only people connected with the system, inmate or professional, to whom a young person can confide fears, and anxieties about abuses. It is important to be clear about what we as workers should do with information imparted to us in these circumstances. The things that we are told in prisons raise many questions and dilemmas for us. Is our client telling us about violations of their rights just to ventilate his feelings or in order that we can use our power and authority to do something about these abuses? We should check this very carefully, because once formal complaints are set in motion evidence and witnesses have a peculiar habit of evaporating. There is also the twist in the tail that prisoners, having no right to due process of law or legal representation in the case of offences allegedly committed against them inside a prison, must take their complaint to the prision's Board of Visitors. Should the witnesses fail to appear, or as sometimes happens, mysteriously change their stories at the last minute, the Board can deduct part of a prisoner's statutory remission for instituting a malicious complaint. Beyond this are the informal sanctions which can be invoked by the subjects of the complaint.

Working for change in the prison

Like the care system the penal system contains a disproportionately number of black prisoners. Research indicates that black young people in the system are more likely to be placed in closed rather than open provision, more likely to lose remission if they are 'found guilty' of disciplinary offences, and more prone to transfer from one goal to another than their white counterparts (Guest, 1984). Psychological survival for black young people in prison concerns not just the preservation of a separate non-institutional self but a black self as well. In the CHE and the prison the question of how our client sustains a positive black identity in a situation in which there is pressure to deny or denigrate his or her blackness will be a paramount concern for social workers. Some institutional regimes attempt to deal with what they identify as the 'problem' of the presence of black youngsters by a policy of dispersal in which they spread black inmates around the institution. As workers working in the interests of individual clients and as members of a profession it is incumbent upon us to ensure, in as much as it is possible, that black young people in care and custody get 'racial support'. Racial support entails creating unrestricted opportunities for black people to associate with each other and to have their dietary and healthcare needs acknowledged and accommodated within the institution. It means ensuring that their religious beliefs and practices are accepted and that provision is made for their celebration. The presence of non-inmate black adult professionals, whether they are prison officers, governors, social workers or clergy can be very important for black young people who are trying to forge an identity for themselves in a situation in which, all too often, being black is seen by those with power in the institution, and some of the inmates as well, as being synonymous with being a prisoner or a client. The provision of alternative role models is an extremely important element in our work with young offenders. The problem for social workers in their dealings with the prison is how to establish the type of relationship with the staff of a prison which will allow them to put these issues 'on the agenda'.

Probation officers in a Youth Custody team in North London initiated a groupwork programme in a Youth Custody Centre (the earlier Borstal) where a large proportion of local young offenders were sent to serve their sentences. The programme was built around the skills necessary for survival in the community but looked as well at survival inside the prison. In these sessions the question of race and racism frequently emerged. The probation officers involved prison officers and assistant governors in the programme but, equally importantly, by dint of being around, they were able to influence thinking in the prison through discussions with staff over lunch or in the bar. It would be wrong to suggest that initiatives of this type are easy, commonplace or an ideal way to address the issue of racism in prisons. It is also the case that the administrative barriers to this type of work confronting social workers in a local authority social services department are fairly formidable. Yet, prisons are not unchanging and unchangable monoliths. Like most other bureaucracies prisons change because circumstances change. The problem for bureaucracies is that often, when they need to change, they don't know what to change or how to change it. The British penal system is full of people who know that the massive influx of black young people demands a serious re-examination of the assumptions which have guided the administration of prisons in the past, but very few of them know how and where to start.

The crisis in British prisons is about aims and objectives as well as bricks and mortar. Staff are unclear about what they are supposed to do, who they are supposed to do it to, and whether it is worth doing anyway. These doubts are compounded by fears of the growing unmanageability of individual penal establishments and the whole system. As such they are in the market for a solution. As we shall see in Chapter 10, social workers can attempt to place themselves, both individually and as a profession, in a position where they can help to find this solution.

10

Working for Change – Political and Administrative Interventions

The juvenile justice strategies advocated by reformers in the 1960s stressed the need for state intervention in the social predicament of the 'delinquent' and professional intervention in his psyche. Welfare and treatment were the weapons with which this assault upon the causes of juvenile crime was to be mounted. The problem of delinquency was located in social disadvantage, and its solution in social reform and social treatment.

The minimalist reaction of the 1970s rejected such social engineering out of hand. For them the 'problem' of juvenile crime was a product of ill-considered social intervention. As a result the best that we could do was to manage social reaction in a way which did not worsen the problem and, wherever and whenever possible, 'leaving the kids alone'.

For all their alleged hard-headedness, *Interventionism* and *Minimalism* both ducked the issue of juvenile crime. Whether viewing it as an innocuous symptom of social disadvantage or a fabrication of heavy-handed agents of social control, juvenile crime was always a symptom of another problem rather than a problem in its own right. Yet, as Lee and Young (1984) observe, 'Working class crime, then, is generated both structurally and culturally within the system; it is part of an individualistic response to this brutalisation created by multiple deprivation. And it then contributes to this brutalisation' (p. 43).

The reluctance of the social democratic Left and the liberal

Centre to come to grips with the lived reality of working-class juvenile crime meant that it fell to the political Right to articulate the predicament of the working-class victim (Wilson, 1975).

Neighbourhood responses to crime, victimisation and the problem of control

Lee and Young raise the problem that the inadequacy of formal and informal responses to working-class juvenile crime compounds the problems of the poor who are, by-and-large, its victims. When people are asked what they consider to be the most pressing problems confronting them, it is the poor, not the rich, who are most likely to put juvenile crime at the top of their list (Wilson, 1975). Paul Harrison (1983) writes:

> But it is not just the facilities that suffer: it is the solidarity of the community itself. Redevelopment, migration and the rapid turnover of people seeking better accommodation means their is precious little of that to start with. But crime dissolves it even further. The climate of fear engenders a defensive egotism of survival in which everyone looks after themselves. A new code of ethics emerges: that thy days be long, thou shalt not question strangers on the stairs; thou shalt not look if thou hears screams or shattering glass; thou shalt not admonish youths for vandalism; thou shalt not help the victim of an attack (p. 282).

The tendencies identified by Paul Harrison are all too real. Yet, contrary to the claims of the political Right, the working-class victims of juvenile crime are not simply asking for more 'law and order'. Jock Young (1987), commenting on responses to a victimisation survey conducted amongst the residents of the Broadwater Farm Estate in North London, writes:

> There was a unity between all sections of the community as to which crimes should be prioritised by the police. . . . Men and women agreed about sexual attacks on women, black and white about racist attacks, old ladies and young blacks about mugging, and the employed and unemployed about burglary. They were critical of the police to be sure, all sections of the community were, but they were not critical of the notion of policing. . . . But these people were (and are) radicals, let us make no mistake about that. They were angry with the police for their corruption, brutality and rank inefficiency; they were fearful of crime and almost universally critical of the politics which had led to mass

unemployment. But there was a consensus within the community, and it had a rational kernel and considerable political potential (p. 22).

In as much as working-class people view juvenile crime as a cause of their problems, they may also identify it as a consequence of the other problems afflicting their neighbourhoods. There is a new politics of juvenile crime emerging in the inner city which welds together a concern with the social and economic conditions which foster crime and victimisation on the one hand, and the effectiveness of the machinery of formal and informal social control on the other. These issues are being reformulated in terms of the overall quality of life in neighbourhoods rather than as atomised encounters between a criminal, a victim and a police officer.

As juvenile crime has become a key political issue for reactionary and progressive Western governments alike, so professional activity in the area has expanded. In the recent period we have witnessed a resurgence of research interest and intervention in the field of environmental crime control and prevention (Newman, 1972; Poyner, 1983; Coleman, 1985). More police officers, private security firms, architects, planners, psychologists and businessmen are involved in the crime control business now than at any other time in the post-war period (South, 1989). Crime in general, and juvenile crime in particular, are big news and big business. When the issue of juvenile crime is linked with the issue of race it is even more certain to remain on the front pages and near the top of central and local government agendas. These initiatives start with a concern for the victim and work backwards to the 'causes' of crime, and forwards to an evaluation of the efficacy of different forms of formal and informal social control (Bright and Petterson, 1984):

A few months ago though, M. Harlem Desir who heads the SOS-Racisme movement with a strong following among immigrants in Les Minguettes revealed the surprising fact that the drain of empty flats had turned round and more people were arriving than leaving. The delinquency rate had dropped from more than 7,200 cases a year to 4,500 and was falling. What had happened?

'Well they had simply done something about the central heating, sound insulation and heat insulation', he said. 'They worked on community equipment, security, sports facilities and job training.' In M. Desir's words racial harmony in concentrated urban development began with improving the quality of the lifts (P. Webster, *Guardian*, 5 September 1988).

The initiative in Les Minguettes and those of the NACRO Safe Neighbourhoods Unit illustrates that in as much as juvenile crime can serve as a divisive force in a neighbourhood it may also be the issue which brings people together to articulate a variety of concerns. In the estates where the NACRO Unit worked the tenants identified repairs, the maintenance of communal areas, caretaking/cleaning, conflict between neighbours and the inadequacy of policing amongst their most pressing concerns (Bright and Petterson, 1984). These neighbourhood approaches to the problem of juvenile crime tend to respond to it as a contributory factor to, and a consequence of, fractured social relationships.

Ramesh's truce

Ramesh was a community worker on an inter-war estate in Inner London. The lower floors of the blocks were largely occupied by white pensioners, some of whom were disabled. The upper floors were mostly occupied by young families of Afro-Caribbean, Cypriot and Asian origin many of whom had teenage children. The youngsters played football and 'hung out' in the courtyard. The elderly residents of the ground floor didn't like the noise they made, not least because they often didn't understand what the youngsters were saying. Many of them were frightened because of what they had heard about black young people in particular and 'foreigners' in general.

One Guy Fawkes night one of the pensioners called the police to the bonfire party in the courtyard. In the ensuing mêlée a police car was turned over and set on fire and five young people were arrested. The police maintained a high profile on the estate after this, partly because some of the pensioners had taken to 'phoning them whenever they were worried.

Ramesh spent time at the lunch club talking about conditions on the estate with the pensioners and time at the youth club doing the same thing with the young people. Both groups appeared to be wholly reasonable, except when it came to talking about each other.

Working very slowly, over a period of months, Ramesh persuaded two representatives of the pensioners and two of the young people to come to a meeting. It emerged at the meeting that both groups were concerned about 'what a dump' the place was becoming. Repairs weren't being done, rubbish wasn't collected, there was nowhere decent outside the flats for the pensioners to sit or for the small children from the upper floors to play.

As to the delicate subject of each other: the pensioners said, and the young people agreed, that it was 'a bit much' if you were sworn at for asking people, who were right outside your window, to keep the noise down. They also agreed that eight o'clock was a reasonable time to stop playing football. The young people said, and the pensioners agreed, that it was 'a bit much' if, just because you were making a bit of a noise, somebody rang the police without even asking you to be quiet.

As a result of this meeting relations between the pensioners and the young people improved a great deal. They talked to each other when they met in the courtyard and some of the pensioners and some of the young people became active in the Tenants Association. Ramesh approached the local police and explained what had happened. The Inspector came to the lunch club to talk to the pensioners who had complained about the young people originally.

The pensioners felt more secure in their flats, the young people felt less 'picked upon', the Tenants Association became stronger, the police returned to a strategy of low-profile policing and arrest rates for juveniles on the estate dropped.

The Safe Neighbourhoods Unit used a similar approach in their detached work programme. This was a response to popular anxieties about the threat posed to person and property by adolescent boys who hung around the estate. These initiatives successfully developed closer links between adults and young people in socially fragmented neighbourhoods. This type of work could lead on to the development of *Young* Tenants Associations described by Robins and Cohen (1978) or the *social* type IT group described by Roger Evans (1982).

> After a lively discusion on this point it was proposed that a film depicting scenes in school should be made. If shown to teachers this might both protect individuals as it came from the group, and it might open up a dialogue with the local schools involved. As far as the staff were concerned the general aims of the video were: firstly to increase collective consciousness about incidents in school and start making an

> analysis of them during the making of the film, secondly to explore alternative ways of handling situations both on the part of the boys and the teachers and in terms of challenging and changing school organisation (p. 34).

These initiatives mark a move beyond educational, recreational or therapeutic responses to young offenders towards the enfranchisement of young people in neighbourhood politics.

Youth and community work reached its zenith in the 1970s only to decline in the 1980s as a consequence of changing political and financial priorities. It is ironical therefore that at the beginning of the 1990s a broad range of professionals, including the police, are turning once again to the knowledge-base and skills of Youth and Community work to flesh out a professional practice which can respond adequately to the problems afflicting the high-crime neighbourhoods of the inner city.

The issue confronting welfare professionals in juvenile justice in the 1990s will increasingly concern the role that they, and their agencies, will play in multi-agency initiatives in high crime areas. Arguably, the emerging practice which draws upon the insights of both *interventionism* and *minimalism*, the victimisation studies of Realist criminology, systems theory and the analysis of the dynamics of power offered by community work, could enable welfare professionals to assume a central role in these initiatives. Their power and importance will, however, probably be determined as much by their political acumen as their professional skills and abilities.

Managing social reaction

At the end-point of the juvenile justice sentencing tariff lies expulsion; the possibility of consignment to the residential and penal institutions which describe the limits of tolerable behaviour of children and young people in England and Wales. As we have noted, these limits are more tightly drawn in Britain than in virtually any other European country, and tighter still if the child or young person is black.

The prison, as the ultimate sanction for non-compliance, gives potency to the lesser penalties a court may impose. It is the threat which lies behind the invitation of IT or supervision. Many workers have found it difficult to work constantly in the shadow of expulsion because, as we have noted, the fatalism engendered by a child or young person's 'internalised tariff' poses a formidable barrier to effective intervention. It is also the case that incarceration tends to make ex-inmates harder to work with afterwards.

Abolitionism

Beyond this professional critique of incarceration, however, lies a political one which is most fully articulated by Thomas Mathiesen (1974). He maintains that imprisonment offers the state a way of making politically inconvenient citizens socially invisible. He argues that in advanced industrial societies continuing political legitimacy requires that the citizens in the mainstream should not be confronted with the harsh realities of life on the margins. During periods of high unemployment therefore, the expulsion to the prison of marginal and potentially disruptive surplus populations offers a means whereby the illusion of social stability and political concensus may be sustained.

As we have seen, in Britain from 1972 onwards the expelled population was increasingly composed of working-class young people in general, and black young people in particular, who had, by dint of their massive over-representation in the unemployment statistics, been redefined politically as 'social dynamite' (Spitzer, 1975).

Mathiesen sees the central task of reform as the reunification of the 'expelled' with the mainstream of the working-class movement. In order to do this, he says, we must build abolitionist alliances which will at first contest, and eventually force the state to abolish imprisonment.

The problem of reform

Would-be reformers of the British juvenile justice system have to confront the unpalatable reality that penal reform is as old as imprisonment itself and has, on the face of it, done little or nothing to reduce its popularity. Mathiesen contends that, historically, the reformers' demands for the minimisation of imprisonment or the abolition of the prison have been met by the rejoinder that they should offer a constructive alternative. They have, as a result, been lured into proposing *positive* reform. These reforms cannot meet all of the objectives of the penal system they are aiming to replace, not least because they fail to offer social invisibility. Instead of the prison being replaced, elements of the reformers schemes' are incorporated into penal regimes as 'humanising influences' and so, far from eroding its power, the reform offers the prison the means to achieve greater legitimacy. The irony of positive reforms is that far from hastening the demise of the prison it serves instead to delay still further its eventual abolition. It is for this reason, Mathiesen suggests, that in our efforts to effect change we should abandon the quest for positive reform in favour of negative reform.

Negative reform contests the power of the penal apparatus and attempts to diminish the credibility and legitimacy of the penal system. The demand for the abolition of solitary confinement in prisons and CHEs, the cessation of enforced drug therapy by the prison medical service and the granting of full civil and legal rights to prisoners all constitute legitimate negative reforms because they require the system to relinquish some of its power over its subjects for them to be realised. Stanley Cohen (1979) has suggested that an abolitionist alliance will adopt a policy of attrition. A gradual process of wearing away in which the realities of the inequality and brutality in our justice system, which is nowhere more evident than in the treatment of black young people, are juxtaposed with the rhetoric which justifies government criminal justice policies.

Mathiesen points to the need to construct both horizontal and vertical alliances. Along the horizontal axis he locates prisoners and ex-prisoners groups, social workers and probation officers, trade-unionists, journalists and academics. The vertical axis rises from the horizontal axis to forge alliances with existing penal pressure groups, politicians at local and national level, groups within political parties concerned with relevant reforms, trades councils, and the trade union movement. Mathiesen's ideas have clear strategic implications for social workers who want to challenge and change the ways juvenile justice is dispensed in England and Wales.

Building alliances within the agency

Effective alliances often start as a result of meetings between social workers and IT workers. The purpose of the meetings may be to explore what people know about the operation of the local juvenile justice system, what they feel about it and what they would like to change about it. This sounds like a very modest beginning but it is alliances which start on the firm basis of proximity, friendship and common interest, and address questions of immediate relevance to our work and the way our own agency operates, which are often the most effective and lasting.

When local authority social services departments have committed themselves to anti-institutional policies in the sphere of juvenile justice it has usually been an alliance of basic grade workers in field work, residential work and IT who have given the initial impetus to the policy and galvinised their higher-status colleagues into action. This has involved a lengthy process of discussion and consultation involving at one end the director of social services who has to present the policy to the council and the chief officers of the other agencies involved in the local juvenile justice system, and at the other, basic grade social workers who have to make the policy work on a day-to-day basis.

Technologies of change

Skynner (1975) and Pincus and Minnahan (1973) alert us to the problem that agencies which are ostensibly committed to helping young offenders may, in fact, constitute a major problem for them. As a result, our target for intervention may well be the structure or functioning of our own 'change-agent system'.

The Lancaster Centre for Youth Crime and Community, as we have noted, has pioneered methods of monitoring and managing the operation of local authority services for young offenders, while JOT has intervened in entire local juvenile justice systems at chief officer level. In their work they have sometimes revealed the ways in which an ostensibly helpful agency, and apparently helpful people, can actually worsen the problem to which they are attempting to be a solution by the imposition of inappropriate labels. David Redmond-Pyle writes:

In all these situations what system studies count is successfully applied labels, i.e. labels which an authorised agency applies and which are not overthrown by alternative definitions of the offence or offender. (For example if a defence solicitor successfully argues that his client is not guilty, the police attempt to catagorise the youngster as an offender fails and the label becomes 'case dismissed'.) The rationale for counting and analysing these successfully applied labels is that, whether or not they reflect the real circumstances of the offending event, and whether or not the Social Enquiry Report or school report accurately portray the 'real' personality, circumstances or conduct of the youngster, these definitions or images play an important part in determining the outcome of the process of juvenile justice. For it is just these labels, these characterisations of the offence and the offender, which form the basis for the magistrates' judgement of what this particular juvenile deserves or needs' (pp. 8–9).

Systems monitoring alerts us to the potential discrepancy between what we believe we are doing and what we are actually doing. Monitoring can be used to analyse who does what to whom in any part of the system. It can be initiated in one office or court or in an entire juvenile justice system. The information supplied by systems monitoring identifies the points in the system where things are going 'wrong' and suggests key points for 'systems intervention'. One research project of this kind revealed that whereas 4 of the 14 juvenile benches monitored accounted for over half of all custodial sentences another five imposed no custodial sentences at all. This finding indicates that different benches in the same court were dispensing different forms of justice, suggesting that the question of equitable sentencing needed to be raised with clerks and magistrates (Lupton and Roberts, 1982).

We have already referred to inter-agency panels created to divert young people away from prosecution. Systems monitoring can provide data with which to identify the key points of intervention. The impetus for cooperation has often come from an alliance of social workers, using systems monitoring data.

Systems monitoring initiatives have been slow to include the racial variable in their analysis and this has seriously limited their usefulness. Questions about the numbers of black youngsters passing through the system, the offences they have committed, their previous offences and the decisions made about them at each stage in the process can yield valuable information about whether, as seems to be the case in certain areas, black and white youngsters follow significantly different trajectories through juvenile justice systems. The introduction of racial monitoring could offer the means whereby concrete targets for anti-racist intervention in the juvenile justice system could be identified.

Systems monitoring would make it possible to identify differential cautioning of black and white offenders or policing methods, like the stop and search, which routinely generate further offences (Pitts, 1986). We might well discover that certain schools are supplying reports to juvenile courts which ensure that black children and young people identified as a problem for the school are being presented to the court in a way which puts them at risk of harsher sentences. A particular bench, or indeed a particular magistrate, may emerge as racially discriminatory and this raises the further question of how we begin to confront the bench about inequitable sentencing.

When informal methods of intervention, like the attempt to confront racially discriminatory sentencing at a magistrates' meeting, are unsuccessful, it may be necessary to formalise the problem and move it up the hierarchy. This, of course, is what hierarchies are for. Magistrates, senior police officers and head teachers can sometimes hear things when they are said by a director or deputy director of social services which they may find incomprehensible on the lips of a basic grade social worker. This is called the 'hierarchy of credibility'. It isn't very nice but it is real and we can use it to our advantage if we have done the groundwork. This groundwork involves the construction of vertical alliances and the development of abolitionist and anti-racist juvenile justice policies within the local authority.

Few local authorities have policies which address the predicament of black children and young people in trouble. When we consider that in some urban areas the majority of young offenders who receive a custodial sentence or are confined in residential care are black, this anomaly is all the more striking.

Workers with black young offenders are in a good position to put their clients' predicament high on the local authority's anti-racist agenda if they have systemic data which includes a racial analysis. The convergence of the issues of juvenile injustice and racism can give added power to their arguments and, perhaps more importantly, broaden the base of the alliance considerably by linking juvenile justice issues, which normally occupy the political margins, with the issue of institutionalised racism which currently occupies centre stage in local authority politics.

An abolitionist, anti-racist, local authority, juvenile justice policy would specify its opposition to residential or custodial confinement for juveniles. It would require changes in the internal operation of the department and in the operation of other agencies as well. It would moreover probably require the appointment, or redesignation, of a worker or workers with responsibility to work with field, residential and IT workers to effect change within and beyond the department. These workers would need access to the social services directorate. If the department wishes to be seen to be acting on behalf, or in the interests, of the black community then one of the roles of an anti-racist juvenile justice worker would be to establish contact with individuals and organisations in that community, with a view to creating a support group or think-tank which could advise the local authority on the development of its juvenile justice policies and provision. This contact would be an important first step in an attempt to develop an abolitionist alliance beyond the local authority, in which some control was vested in the hands of the people who have the greatest interest in effecting change in the British juvenile justice system, namely those who are, have been, or are in danger of being 'expelled'.

Building alliances with the expelled

Important though affiliation to, or alliances with, organisations of professionals and reformers may be, it is essential that any abolitionist alliance retains its links with its primary constituency, the expelled. Professionals involved in reform are notorious for failing to involve the intended benificiaries in the process of change. What Mathiesen advocates, and NAYPIC exemplifies, is the importance of working with the oppressed and the expelled to define aims, objectives, tactics and strategies. How often do social workers, IT workers or probation officers approach black churches or black cultural and self-help organisations to hear about the problems that black parents and their children face when they become involved in the juvenile justice system? Almost thirty years on we continue to fall into the trap described by Robert F. Kennedy when he spoke of the relationship between welfare professionals and those on whose behalf they claim to be working:

'They plan for the poor, not with them. Part of the sense of helplessness and futility comes from the feeling of powerlessness to affect the operation of these organisations' (Moynihan, 1969, pp. 90–1).

NAYPIC, which has been successful in organising groups of young people in care and developing a charter of rights, has shown how strong and vocal alliances can be established between expelled institutional populations, ex-inmates of those institutions and welfare professionals. It has pursued causes and taken up cases and in doing so has used the media and adult support groups without sacrificing control of the direction of its campaign. The main source of its strength remains children and young people who are, or have recently been, in care themselves.

Building alliances beyond the agency

Some of the most pressing issues concerning children and young people in the local juvenile justice system cannot be addressed through the action or agitation of social workers within their own agency. As we have already noted the question of the differential policing and sentencing of black youngsters are the cases *par excellence* of the need to make alliances beyond our own agency, and eventually beyond the level of local politics as well, if real change is to be effected. We will therefore need to consider the organisations with which we can establish productive alliance.

It is not possible to specify the particular organisation or group which will act as a vehicle for change in any given place at any given time. It is a question of identifying the grouping or groupings which, at a particular point, have both the energy and the acumen to act as a vehicle for change. The NALGO branch, the social workers' lunch club, the Community Relations Council, the BASW branch, the local IT Association, the local branch of the Association of Black Social Workers, the Borough Youth Forum, a group formed by a consortium of local churches or a Police Accountability Group can all give the impetus to, and serve as vehicles for change. The process by which we select the best group for the job will depend ultimately upon political judgement, availability and luck.

Conclusion

On the face of it, a 'law and order' era is a bad time in which to develop positive social work practice with young offenders and negative penal reform. In 1969 the government introduced Intermediate Treatment and the 'Poverty Programme' as a means of compensating disadvantaged youngsters and diverting them from care and custody. In 1989 the government introduced *Punishment, Custody and the Community* which, through the use of electronic tagging, threatens to turn the young offender's home into an adjunct of the prison.

In the past few years workers with young offenders have not felt very important. They have been eclipsed professionally by colleagues doing much more fashionable things like family therapy and they have been marginalised politically by a government which has lampooned them for not being tough enough. Yet, as we have seen, it is social workers, IT and Youth workers who are devising some of the most effective strategies for combatting two of the government's most pressing domestic problems.

The problems of social relations in the inner city and the crisis in the prison have not been responsive to the government's 'common sense' policies. Judges and magistrates have ignored their exhortations to 'go easy' on offenders. The 'trickle-down effect', in which money given to the rich is somehow supposed to improve the quality of life of the poor, has been ineffective. As a result, in the early 1990s it is once again the ideas and practices developed within social welfare which are being discussed in the upper echelons of government and the police force.

When British governments do the 'right thing' about juvenile justice they almost invariably do it for the 'wrong' reasons. Despite the financial assault upon local authorities and the voluntary sector, and the ideological assault upon social work, resources for social work with young offenders are increasing. This is not a result of sentimentality on the part of the government but a realisation that when their rhetoric has run its course it may be necessary to turn to the professionals for a solution.

Suggestions for Further Reading

Who are Young Offenders?

A necessary prelude to effective work with children and young people in trouble is the attempt to understand how it would feel to be in their predicament. We can go some way towards this by reading factual and fictional accounts of what it is like to be young and in trouble.

Novels

J. D. Salinger's *Catcher in the Rye* (1951) is the brilliant prototype of tales about a young person trying to find a place for himelf in a corrupt and irrational adult world. Holden Caulfield began to 'ask himself it it's him or them that's really insane' when Bob Dylan was in primary school and James Dean was rehearsing for his first acting role as John the Apostle. Carson Maculler's *The Heart is a Lonely Hunter* is a beautiful study of a girl growing up amidst bigotry, hatred and ignorance. Alan Sillitoe's *The Loneliness of the Long Distance Runner* and Brendan Behan's autobiographical *Borstal Boy* both tell us how young people deal with the experience of imprisonment. F. Scott Fitzgerald's short story *Winter Dreams* and Philip Roth's *Portnoy's Complaint* offer contrasting and vivid accounts of adolescent love and sexuality. These are all books about adolescents written for adults. One of the authors who is read most avidly *by* children and young people, however, is Judy Blume. Her characters confront real problems like under-age sex, divorce, sibling rivalry and racism and she deals frankly with issues which many adults would prefer not to discuss with children and young people. Try the children's story *Iggie's House*, and *Tiger Eyes*, which was written for young adults. Children and young people identify with the characters she creates and as a result they write to her about their problems. Some of the thousands of letters she has received are published in *Letters to Judy: What Kids Wish They Could Tell You* (London: Pan, 1987).

Non-fiction

W. F. Whyte's *Street Corner Society* (University of Chicago Press, 1943), is the classic 'participant observation' study. The value of these studies is that, more than any other form of social research, they allow the subject to 'tell it like it is' and this makes them invaluable for our purposes. In Britain in the 1970s and 1980s participant observation, or ethnography as it came to be called, underwent a renaissance. Of particular importance are: Howard Parker's *A View From the Boys: A Sociology of Downtown Adolescents* (Newton Abbot: David and Charles, 1974); Paul Willis's *Learning to Labour: How Working Class Kids Get Working Class Jobs* (London: Saxon House, 1977); Ken Pryce's *Endless Pressure* (Harmondsworth: Penguin, 1979); Paul Corrigan's 'Doing Nothing' in Stuart Hall and Tony Jefferson (eds) *Resistance Through Rituals* (London: Hutchinson, 1976), and Geoffrey Pearson's *The New Heroin Users* (Oxford: Blackwell, 1987).

Alice Miller's *The Drama of Being a Child* (London: Virago, 1987) gives an insight into the ways bright children survive maddening families. *Social Work with Black Children and their Families*, S. Ahmed *et al.* (eds) (London: Batsford, 1986), offers a good introduction to the problems and issues confronted by black youngsters in their dealings with social workers and some of the things which can be done about it.

1. The Politics of Policy

I have considered the relationship between politics, policy and practice in greater depth in J. Pitts (1988), *The Politics of Juvenile Crime*. John Clarke's (1980) 'Social Democratic Delinquents and Fabian Families', in *National Deviancy Conference Permissiveness and Control* (London: Macmillan) is an important contribution, as is Anthony Bottoms's 'On the Decriminalisation of the English Juvenile Court', in R. Hood (ed.) *Crime, Criminology and Public Policy* (London: Heinemann, 1974). Ian Taylor was one of the first people on the Left to respond to the 'justice' lobby's critique of welfarism. See his *Law and Order – Arguments for Socialism* (London: Macmillan, 1981), not least for its response to the provocative, if at times confused, *Delinquent Fantasies* of Patricia Morgan (London: Maurice Temple Smith, 1978).

2. Negative Practice

The argument for 'leaving the kids alone' is persuasively stated in Edwin Schur's *Radical Non-Intervention* (London: Prentice-Hall, 1973). An equally persuasive rejoinder comes from Stan Cohen in 'It's Alright for You to Talk', in R. Bailey and M. Brake (eds) *Radical Social Work* (London: Edward Arnold, 1980), who sees in radical non-intervention the danger that we might neglect the needs of the socially deprived offender.

Coming from a very different political position from Schur, James Q. Wilson in *Thinking About Crime* (New York: Basic Books, 1975) also questions the efficacy of social intervention with offenders and argues instead for the incapacitation of persistent offenders for lengthy periods in order to protect their working class victims. John Lea and Jock Young in *What is to be Done About Law and Order?* (Harmondsworth: Penguin, 1984) develop this argument, suggesting that for too long the political Left has ignored the fact that crime is a real problem for the working-class and not just a figment of the right-wing imagination. In *The Politics of Juvenile Crime* (London: Sage, 1988), I attempt to reconcile the 'Left-Realist' concern with the socially deprived victim of juvenile crime and the abiding problem of the social deprivation of many young offenders.

3. Towards a New Paradigm for Positive Practice

John Lea and Jock Young offer a penetrating account of the political significance of the disturbances of 1981 and the relationship between crime policing and political unrest in *What Is To Be Done About Law and Order?* I have summarised research on racism in the juvenile justice system in J. Pitts 'Black Youth and Crime: Some Unanswered Questions', in R. Matthews and J. Young (eds) *Confronting Crime* (London: Sage, 1986). The chapter entitled 'The Great Taboo: Men's Dependency' in *What Do Women Want?* by Luise Eichenbaum and Susie Orbach, (London: Fontana, 1983), offers us an insight into the difficulties men have with their emotions and some clues about how we might begin to approach working with them. Geoff Pearson's *The New Heroin Users* (Oxford: Blackwell, 1987) offers eloquent testimony to the fact that heroin abuse is essentially a social and economic problem and not a question of personal weakness or individual pathology. Edwin Lemert's 'Juvenile Justice Italian Style', *Law and Society Review* (1986), vol. 20, no. 4, offers us a refreshing glimpse of progressive reform in a country which has a juvenile justice system somewhat similar to our own.

4. The Juvenile Justice System

Malcolm Klein's (1984) *Western Systems of Juvenile Justice* is not the most riveting book in this field but it does offer an opportunity to gain a new perspective on our own system by comparing it with those of other nations. Keith Bottomley and Ken Pease have brought together a wealth of statistical material in a very comprehensible way in their (1986) *Crime and Punishment – Interpreting the Data*. David Matza's study of the juvenile court in *Delinquency and Drift* (London: John Wiley, 1964) remains a classic and opened the way for numerous other studies of the unintended consequences of ostensibly benign intentions, of which David Thorpe *et al.*, *Out of Care* (London: Allen and Unwin, 1980) is a recent British example.

5. Making an Assessment and Planning an Intervention

Charles Critcher's 'Structures, Cultures and Biographies' in Stuart Hall and Tony Jefferson's *Resistance through Rituals*, offers us a useful conceptual framework with which to understand juvenile offending and young offenders. In *Endless Pressure* (Harmondsworth: Penguin, 1979) Ken Pryce offers a fascinating analysis of the specific structural, cultural and biographical factors which predispose the young people he writes about to crime. What Ken Pryce does for race, Jean Gregory does for gender. In her 'Sex, Class and Crime: Towards a Non-sexist Criminology', in R. Matthews and J. Young, *Confronting Crime*, she considers gender differences in patterns of offending and processing through the justice system and alerts us to the ways in which gender socialisation might contribute to a young person's offending.

John Holt, in *Why Children Fail* (Harmondsworth: Penguin, 1969), utilises an interactionist perspective to explain why a majority of young people leave school believing that they are failures. In a similar vein R. D. Laing in *The Politics of the Family* (Harmondsworth: Penguin) describes how the 'identified patient' is inducted into the mad role by his or her family.

Robin Skynner's 'The Minimum Sufficient Network' in *Social Work Today*, August 1971, offers us a solid conceptual basis for planning our intervention. Taken together with the work of A. Pincus and A. Minahan, *Social Work Practice, Model and Method* (Illinois: Peacock Press, 1973), we have a useful model for locating our client within the systems which generate the problem and might be mobilised as part of the solution.

6. Working with the Court

Receiving Juvenile Justice (Oxford: Blackwell, 1981) by Howard Parker, Maggie Casburn and Dave Turnbull is probably the best account available of the ways in which juvenile courts actually operate. It demonstrates convincingly that the 'justice' young offenders receive is a consequence not so much of what they do, but rather of where they do it. *Social Work and The Courts* edited by Howard Parker (London: Edward Arnold, 1979) is a useful collection of informative yet critical papers on the functioning, and malfunctioning, of courts, and social workers in them. Pat Carlen and Margaret Powell's ironic and thought-provoking contribution to this volume. *Professionals in the Magistrates' Courts: the Courtroom Lore of Probation Officers and Social Workers* should not be missed. Margaret Powell's 'Court Work', in H. Walker and B. Beaumont, *Working with Offenders*, gives a practical guide to working in this often difficult setting without sacrificing either our integrity or our compassion.

Preparation for Placement by Henry Ross (Newcastle upon Tyne Polytechnic Products Ltd, 1986) is designed for students embarking on a probation placement and it tells you all the things you most needed to know but felt silly about asking. It explains the terms used in the justice system, the penalties which can be imposed, and the rights and responsibilities of the system professionals. With this little book in your pocket you will probably feel a lot more confident about your practice. An even smaller, more rudimentary, but equally useful publication is *The Social Enquiry Report – and How to Frame It* (1984) published by the Devon Probation Service, which, as its title implies, tells you very simply how to frame a Social Inquiry Report. *The Sentence of the Court* (London: HMSO, 1986) gives a brief but interesting account of the powers available to courts and some helpful comments on how they use them. Andrew Ashworth's *Sentencing and Penal Policy* (London: Weidenfeld and Nicolson, 1983) offers a more substantial analysis of the relationship between the choices made by judges and magistrates and the intentions of government.

7. Direct Work with Young Offenders in the Community

There are a number of useful books which deal specifically with social work with children and young people. See particularly: R. Jones and C. Pritchard, *Social Work with Adolescents* (London: Routledge, 1986); S. Martell, *Direct Work with Children* (London: Family Service Unit, 1983); and F. Lieberman, *Social Work with Children* (Human Sciences Press, 1979). E. Holgate (ed.), *Communicating with Children* (London: Longman, 1972) is an important accompaniment to these works.

Two of the most useful books about Social Groupwork are Saul Bernstein's (ed.) *Explorations in Groupwork* (1965), and *Further Explorations in Group Work* (1970) (Boston University Press). Tom Douglas's *Groupwork Practice* (London: Tavistock, 1976) is a useful British text and P. Priestly *et al.*, *Social Skills in Prison and the Community* (Routledge & Kegan Paul, 1984) is a good introduction to social skills groups. The 'offending workshop' is introduced in D. Thorpe *et al.*, *Out of Care* (London: Allen and Unwin, 1980) and these ideas are developed in Lucy Ball and Theo Sowa's *Groupwork and I.T.* (London: London Intermediate Treatment Association, 1985). Work with 'natural' peer groups of young people in trouble was never done more thoroughly than in *The Wincroft Youth Project* by C. Smith, M. Farrant and H. Marchant (London: Tavistock, 1972). Many of S. Minuchin's theories were developed in his work with young offenders and their families. See his *Families and Family Therapy* (Cambridge, Mass.: Harvard University Press, 1974).

8. Indirect Work with Young Offenders in the Community

J. Cheetham *et al.*, *Social and Community Work in a Multi-Racial Society* (London: Harper and Row, 1981) offers a useful insight into the issues which concern youth and community workers and the ways in which they work. *The Wincroft Youth Project* shows something of the uncertainties and rewards of detached youth work. *Knuckle Sandwich* by Dave Robbins and Phil Cohen (Harmondsworth: Penguin, 1978) draws upon work undertaken in a youth project in North London to examine the extent to which Youth Work can be a radical, or radicalising, force. Michael Rutter *et al.*'s, *Fifteen Thousand Hours* (London: Open Books, 1978) has important implications for school-based work with young offenders. Robert Adams *et al.*, *A Measure of Diversion* (Leicester: National Youth Bureau, 1981) is a useful introduction to activities subsumed under the heading Intermediate Treatment as is S. Curris, *Delinquency Prevention through Intermediate Treatment* (London: Batsford). *The Politics of Juvenile Crime* I offer a historical analysis of its development.

9. Working with Young Offenders in Care and Custody

Nigel Stone's 'Prison Work' in H. Walker and B. Beaumont *Working with Offenders* (1985) gives a useful account of the problems of being inside. For a more detailed account of the ways in which people defend themselves from the effects of imprisonment and other unpalatable social realities see S. Cohen and L. Taylor, *Escape Attempts* (London: Allen Lane, 1978). The contribution of social work intervention to the eventual incarceration of children and young people is dealt with by S. Millham *et al.*, *Locking Up Children* (London: Saxon House, 1978) and H. A. Thomas, 'The Road to Custody is Paved with Good Intentions', *Probation Journal*, vol. 29, no. 3. The effects of separation are considered by V. Falhberg, *Helping Children When They Must Move* (London: British Agencies for Adoption and Fostering) and C. J. Jewett *Helping Children to Cope with Separation and Loss* (London: Batsford, British Agencies for Adoption and Fostering, 1984).

10. Working for Change – Political and Administrative

Thomas Mathiesen's *The Politics of Abolition* (London: Martin Robertson, 1974) is essential reading for any would-be penal reformer but so is 'Abolition Possibilities and Pitfalls' by David Downes in A. E. Bottoms and R. H. Preston, *The Coming Penal Crisis* (Edinburgh: Scottish Academic Press, 1980). Bill Beaumont explores the possibilities of change in the probation service in 'Probation: Working for Social Change' in H. Walker and B. Beaumont (eds) *Working with Offenders*. Saul Alinsky is the man who all but turned political agitation into an art form. Read his thoughtful and funny *Rules for Radicals* (New York: Random House, 1972).

References

Ahmed, S. (1986) 'Cultural Racism in Work with Women and Girls' in S. Ahmed *et al.*, *Social Work with Black Children and their Families*, London, Batsford.

Alinsky, S. (1974) *Rules for Radicals*, New York, Vintage.

Bateson, G. (1972) *Steps to an Ecology of Mind*, New York, Ballantine.

Booker, C. (1980) *The Seventies*, Harmondsworth, Penguin.

Berlins, M. and Wansell, G. (1974) *Caught in the Act*, Harmondsworth, Penguin.

Berry, S. (1984) *Ethnic Minorities and the Juvenile Court*, Nottinghamshire Social Services Department.

Bottomley, K. and Pease, K. (1986) *Crime and Punishment – Interpreting the Data*, Milton Keynes, Open University Press.

Bottoms, A. E. (1974) 'On the Decriminalisation of the English Juvenile Court' in R. Hood (ed.) *Crime, Criminology, and Public Policy*, London: Heinemann, pp. 319–45.

Bottoms, A. E. (1977) 'Reflections on the Renaissance of Dangerousness', *Howard Journal*, 16 (2) pp. 70–96.

Box, S. (1983) *Power, Crime and Mystification*, London, Tavistock.

Box, S. and Hale, C. (1986) 'Unemployment, Crime and the Enduring Problem of Prison Overcrowding' in R. Matthews and J. Young, *Confronting Crime*, London, Sage.

Brewer, C. and Lait, J. (1980) *Can Social Work Survive?*, London, Temple Smith.

Bright, J. and Petterson, G. (1984) *The Safe Neighbourhoods Unit*, London, NACRO.

Burney, E. (1979) *Magistrate, Court and Community*, London, Hutchinson.

Capra, F. (1982) *The Turning Point*, London, Flamingo.

Carlen, P. (1983) 'On Rights and Powers' in D. Garland and P. Young, *The Power to Punish*, London, Heinemann.

Cashmore, E. and Troyna, B. (eds) (1982) *Black Youth in Crisis*, London, Allen and Unwin.

Cawson, P. and Martell, P. (1979) *Children Referred to Closed Units*, London, DHSS.

Chard, A., Dennington, J., Eyres, R., Farrel, M. and Green, C. (1983) *The Appeal Process and the Juvenile Justice System*, London, National Intermediate Treatment Federation.
Cloward, R. and Ohlin, L. (1960) *Delinquency and Opportunity*, London, Routledge.
Cornish, D. B. and Clarke, R. V. G. (1975) *Residential Treatment and its Effects on Delinquency*, London, Home Office.
Critcher, C. (1975) 'Structures, Cultures and Biographies' in S. Hall and T. Jefferson (eds) *Resistance Through Rituals*, London, Hutchinson.
Cicourel, A. V. (1968) *The Social Organisation of Juvenile Justice*, New York, Wiley.
Cohen, S. (1979) *How Do We Balance Guilt, Justice and Tolerance?*, London, Radical Alternatives to Prison.
Cohen, S. (1980) 'It's Alright for You to Talk' in R. Bailey and M. Brake (eds) *Radical Social Work*, London, Edward Arnold.
Cohen, S. (1983) 'Social Control Talk' in D. Garland and P. Young (eds) *The Power to Punish*, London, Heinemann.
Coleman, A. (1985) *Utopia on Trial*, London, Hilary Shipman.
De La Motta, C. (1984) *Blacks in the Criminal Justice System*, unpublished MSc thesis, University of Aston.
Demuth, C. (1978) *SUS: A Report on the Vagrancy Act 1824*, London, Runnymede Trust.
DHSS (1985) *Social Work Decisions In Child Care*, London, HMSO.
Dodd, D. (1978) 'Police and Thieves on the Streets of Brixton', *New Society*, 16 March.
Douglas, T. (1970) *A Decade of Small Group Theory*, London, Bookstall Publications.
Eichenbaum, L. and Orbach, S. (1984) *What Do Women Want?*, London, Fontana.
Evans, R. (1982) *The Theoretical Foundations of Doing IT*, Norwich, University of East Anglia.
Farrington, D. (1985) 'England and Wales' in M. Klein (ed.) *Western Systems of Juvenile Justice*, London, Sage.
Goffman, I. (1968) *Asylums*, Harmondsworth, Penguin.
Gregory, J. (1986) 'Sex, Class and Crime: Towards a Non-Sexist Criminology' in R. Matthews and J. Young (eds) *Confronting Crime*, London, Sage.
Guest, C. (1984) *A Comparative Analysis of the Career Patterns of Black and White Young Offenders*, unpublished MSc, thesis, Cranfield Institute.
Hall, S. and Jefferson, T. (1976) *Resistance through Rituals*, London, Hutchinson.
Hall, S., Clarke, J., Crichter, C., Jefferson, T. and Roberts, B. (1978) *Policing the Crisis*, London, Macmillan.
Hargreaves, D. (1967) *Social Relations in the Secondary School*, London, Routledge.
Harris, T. (1971) *Survey of Immigrants in Approved Schools*, unpublished, London, DHSS.

Harrison, P. (1983) *Inside the Inner City: Life Under the Cutting Edge*, Harmondsworth, Penguin.
Heap, K. (1968) 'The Social Group Worker as Central Person', *British Journal of Social Work*, vol. 25, no. 1, pp. 20–9.
HMSO (1968) *Children in Trouble*, Cmnd. 3601, London.
Home Office (1984) *Tougher Regimes in Detention Centres*, London, HMSO.
Hugman, B. (1974) *Act Natural*, London, NCVO.
Jones, D. (1987) *Understanding Child Abuse*, London, Macmillan.
Jones, T., Maclean, B. and Young, J. *The Islington Crime Survey*, Aldershot, Gower.
Kettle, M. (1982) 'The Racial Numbers Game In Our Prisons', *New Society*, September.
King, M. and May, C. (1985) *Black Magistrates*, London, Cobden Trust.
King, M. (1987) *Social Prevention in France*, London, NACRO.
Klein, M. (1984) *Western Systems of Juvenile Justice*, London, Sage.
Laing, R. D. and Esterton, A. (1967) *Sanity, Madness and the Family*, Harmondsworth, Penguin.
Landau, S. (1981) 'Juveniles and the Police', *British Journal of Criminology*, 21, pp. 143–72.
Lawrence, M. (1983) '. . . It's Different for Girls . . .' in *Eureka*, Journal of the London Intermediate Treatment Association, Autumn.
Lee, J. and Young, J. (1984) *What is to be Done About Law and Order?*, Harmondsworth, Penguin.
Lemert, E. (1986) 'Juvenile Justice Italian Style', *Law and Society Review*, vol. 20, no. 4.
Martin, D. (1985) *Afro-Caribbean Clients in Youth Custody*, unpublished, S.E. London Probation Service Survey.
Mathiesen, T. (1965) *The Defences of the Weak*, London, Tavistock.
Mathiesen, T. (1974) *The Politics of Abolition*, London, Martin Robertson.
Matza, D. (1964) *Delinquency and Drift*, New York, Wiley.
Mead, G. H. (1934) *Mind, Self and Society From the Standpoint of a Social Behaviourist*, University of Chicago Press.
Millham, S. (1977) 'Intermediate Treatment – Symbol or Solution?', *Youth in Society*, 26, pp. 22–4.
Millham, S., Bullock, R. and Hosie, K. (1978) *Locking Up Children*, Farnborough, Saxon House.
Mills, C. W. (1959) *The Sociological Imagination*, Oxford University Press.
Minuchin, S. (1974) *Families and Family Therapy*, London, Tavistock.
Moynihan, D. P. (1969) *Maximum Feasible Misunderstanding*, New York, Free Press.
Morgan, P. (1978) *Delinquent Fantasies*, London, Temple Smith.
Morris, A., Giller, H., Szwed, E. and Geach, H. (1980) *Justice for Children*, London, Macmillan.
NACRO (1984) *School Reports in the Juvenile Court*, London.
NACRO (1986) *NACRO Briefing*, London.

NACRO (1987) *Diverting Juveniles From Custody*, London.
Newman, O. (1972) *Defensible Space*, New York, Macmillan.
Ohlin, L. (1979) 'The American Experience' in DHSS (ed.) *Getting On With I.T.*, London.
Parker, H., Casburn, M. and Turnbull, D. (1980) 'The Production of Punitive Juvenile Justice', *British Journal of Criminology*, 20 (3).
Pearson, G. (1987) *The New Heroin Users*, Oxford, Blackwell.
Pincus, A. and Minahan, A. (1973) *Social Work Practice, Model and Method*, Illinois, Peacock Press.
Pinder, R. (1983) *Dealing in Diversity*, unpublished.
Pitts, J., Sowa, T., Taylor, A. and Whyte, L. (1986) 'Developing an Anti-Racist Intermediate Treatment' in S. Ahmed *et al.* (eds) *Social Work with Black Children and their Families*, London, Batsford.
Pitts, J. (1986) 'Black Young People and Juvenile Crime. Some Unanswered Questions' in R. Matthews and J. Young (eds) *Confronting Crime*, London, Sage.
Pitts, J. (1988) *The Politics of Juvenile Crime*, London, Sage.
Powell, M. (1985) 'Court Work' in H. Walker and B. Beaumont (eds) *Working with Offenders*, London, Macmillan.
Power, M. J., Benn, R. T. and Norris, J. N. (1972) 'Neighbourhood, School, and Juveniles Before the Courts', *British Journal of Criminology*, 12, pp. 111–32.
Poyner, B. (1983) *Design Against Crime*, London, Butterworths.
Priestley, P., McGuire, J., Flegg, D., Hemsley, V., Welham, D. and Barnett, R. (1984) *Social Skills in Prison and the Community*, London, Routledge.
Pryce, K. (1979) *Endless Pressure*, Harmondsworth, Penguin.
Redmond-Pyle, D. (1982) *Investigating the Local Juvenile Criminal Justice System*, Lancaster, Centre of Youth Crime and Community.
Reid, W. J. and Shyne, A. W. (1969) *Brief and Extended Casework*, New York, Columbia University Press.
Robins, D. and Cohen, P. (1978) *Knuckle Sandwich*, Harmondsworth, Penguin.
Reinach, E., Lovelock, R. and Roberts, G. (1974) *First Year at Fairfield Lodge*, Portsmouth Polytechnic Social Services Intelligence Unit.
Rosenthal, R. (1968) *Pygmalion in the Classroom – Teacher Expectation and Pupil's Intellectual Development*, New York, Holt, Rinehart and Winston.
Rutherford, A. (1986) *Growing Out of Crime*, Harmondsworth, Penguin.
Rutter, M., Maughan, B., Mortimore, P., Ouson, J. and Smith, A. (1978) *Fifteen Thousand Hours*, London, Open Books.
Satir, V. (1964) *Conjoint Family Therapy*, Palo Alto, Science and Behaviour Books.
Schur, E. (1974) *Radical Non-Intervention*, New York, Prentice-Hall.
Skynner, R. (1971) 'The Minimum Sufficient Network', *Social Work Today*, August.
Smith, C., Farrant, M. and Marchant, H. (1972) *The Wincroft Youth Project*, London, Tavistock.

Smith, D. (1983) *Police and People in London*, London, Policy Studies Institute.

South, N. (1989) *Policing for Profiit*, London, Sage.

Spitzer, S. (1975) 'Towards a Marxian Theory of Crime', *Social Problems*, 22, pp. 368–401.

Stevens, P. and Willis, C. (1979) *Race, Crime and Arrests*, London, Home Office.

Stone, N. (1985) 'Prison-Based Work' in H. Walker and B. Beaumont (eds) *Working with Offenders*, London, Macmillan.

Taylor, I., Walton, P. and Young, J. (1973) *The New Criminology*, London, Routledge.

Taylor, I. (1981) *Law and Order Arguments for Socialism*, London, Macmillan.

Taylor, W. (1981) *Probation and Aftercare in a Multi-Racial Society*, London, CRE and West Midlands Probation and Aftercare Service.

Taylor, W. (1982) 'Black Youth, White Man's Justice', *Youth in Society*, November 14–17.

Thorpe, D., Smith, D., Green, C. and Paley, J. *Out of Care*, London, Allen and Unwin.

Tipler, J. (1985) *Juvenile Justice in Hackney*, Hackney Social Services Department.

Webster, P. (1988) 'A Community Growing From the Rubble', *Guardian*, 5 September.

Whyte, W. F. (1943) *Street Corner Society*, University of Chicago Press.

Willis, P. (1977) *Learning to Labour*, London, Saxon House.

Wilson, J. Q. (1975) *Thinking About Crime*, New York, Basic Books.

Young, J. (1987) 'The Tasks Facing a Realist Criminology', *Contemporary Crises*, vol. 11, 337–56.

Zander, M. (1975) 'What Happens to Young Offenders in Care?', *New Society*, 24 June.

Index